SOLDIER, SISTER, SPY, SCOUT

OTHER BOOKS BY CHRIS ENSS AND JOANN CHARTIER

Love Untamed
She Wore a Yellow Ribbon

SOLDIER, SISTER, SPY, SCOUT

Women Soldiers and Patriots on the Western Frontier

CHRIS ENSS AND JoANN CHARTIER

TWODOT®

GUILFORD, CONNECTICUT
HELENA, MONTANA

A · TWODOT® · BOOK

An imprint and registered trademark of Rowman & Littlefield

Distributed by NATIONAL BOOK NETWORK

British Library Cataloguing-in-Publication Information Available

Library of Congress Cataloging-in-Publication Data

Names: Enss, Chris, 1961- author. | Chartier, JoAnn, author.
Title: Soldier, sister, spy, scout : women soldiers and patriots on the
  Western frontier / Chris Enss and JoAnn Chartier.
Other titles: Women soldiers and patriots on the Western frontier
Description: Guilford, Connecticut : TwoDot, [2016] | Includes
  bibliographical references.
Identifiers: LCCN 2015041791 (print) | LCCN 2015046491 (ebook) | ISBN
  9781493023394 (pbk.) | ISBN 9781493023400 (e-book)
Subjects: LCSH: Women pioneers—West (U.S.)—Biography. | Women
  soldiers—West (U.S.)—Biography. | Frontier and pioneer life—West
  (U.S.). | West (U.S.)—Biography.
Classification: LCC F596 .E58 2016 (print) | LCC F596 (ebook) | DDC
  920.72—dc23
LC record available at http://lccn.loc.gov/2015041791

CONTENTS

Acknowledgments

The authors are grateful for the assistance of staff at the following institutions: Nevada Historical Society; University of Nevada Reno; California State History Library; National Archives and Records Administration; Texas State Archives; Barker History Center, University of Texas, Austin; Colorado Historical Society; Michigan Historical Society; Kansas Historical Society; and Nevada County Public Library.

Special thanks to Colin MacKenzie at the Nautical Research Center, Petaluma, California; Maria Brower at the Doris Foley History Library, Nevada City, California; Suzanne Moody at the Chiricahua National Monument Visitor Center; Nancy Jennings at the Johnson County Library in Buffalo, Wyoming; Kathleen Fletcher at Klamath County Museum; Julie Parry for her input and critique of the work; Cynthia Martin for her artistic expertise and friendship; and Erin Turner and Jan Cronan for their support and skills as editors.

And especially to Becky Habblett for the lighthouse ladies: Your light still shines.

INTRODUCTION

FROM THE EARLIEST DAYS OF STORYTELLING, THE COURAGEOUS MAN has been celebrated in myth and legend. Every culture develops stories about dauntless adventurers, valiant patriots, fearless warriors, and heroic leaders. These stories teach as well as entertain and set up positive role models to inspire future generations. Sometimes, these dauntless, valiant, fearless, and heroic individuals are women.

The true stories you'll find in this book about women in the American West illustrate the depth of courage, the physical bravery, and the commitment to a cause that impelled them to throw off the constraints of nineteenth-century conventions and plunge into situations that many men of their era would not, and did not, face.

In the latter half of the nineteenth century, the US Army battled western Native American tribes over territorial rights, resources, and culture. Each side had its motives, its victories, its defeats, its victims, and its heroes. Among those heroes, on both sides, were women—wives, mothers, interpreters, laundresses, soldiers, and shamans—who willingly headed into the unknown, into a land fraught with danger and hardship. *Courageous* defines the character of the thousands of women who left the towns and cities of the East for the unknown dangers of the western territories. Setting up housekeeping in wild, unsettled lands, risking their lives on the journey, and bearing children under primitive conditions tested their courage daily. The stories selected for this book describe some who went two or three steps beyond the ordinary, everyday courage of women in the West.

Some of these women not only did a man's job in war, but also did it without ever revealing a then unacceptable truth—that they were members of the "fairer sex." *Soldier, Sister, Spy, Scout: Women Soldiers and Patriots on the Western Frontier* celebrates women such as Buffalo Soldier Cathy Williams, who served in the Thirty-eighth Infantry for nearly two years without revealing her gender. As a civilian in 1868, she put away her uniform and tied her hair back with a yellow ribbon to show her fellow soldiers that she was proud to be a woman. Rarely recognized for courage were devoted wives and mothers, such as Elizabeth Custer, wife of General George Custer. A slender woman of genteel breeding, Elizabeth defied convention of the day and traveled with her husband throughout the unsettled plains, living in military encampments and covered wagons, nursing troops, and enduring hardships as a military frontier wife.

The bravery and compassion of two Mexican women caught in the Mexican War's battles at the Alamo and Goliad are included, along with the counterpoint view provided by an eighteen-year-old bride on her honeymoon journey down the Santa Fe Trail just as that war began. The little-known stories of three Native American women who faced death to save their people show that bravery was not just a male attribute. Even notorious women such as Calamity Jane exhibited an astonishing level of courage in completely unexpected settings.

To help settle the expanding boundaries of an emerging nation, all of these women endured fierce extremes of climate, rigorous overland travel, lack of food and water at times, and the constant threat of death to themselves and their loved ones. *Soldier, Sister, Spy, Scout: Women Soldiers and Patriots on the Western Frontier* profiles more than a dozen daring women who were unrecognized in their time. Even today some people doubt their courage.

When reading biased, untruthful, and deliberately inflammatory newspaper editorials of 1875 about Paiute heroine Sarah Winnemucca, for instance, it's easy to say, "That was then, this is now, and people don't belittle and demean women anymore." Today, most historians are proud of the information they can provide about these heroic women. While researching these stories, however, we were surprised to discover that a few men guarding the heritage of the past in museums and archives discounted the accomplishments of certain women we've included in this book. Sally Zanjani, in her biography of Sara Winnemucca, recounts events in a Nevada town that raucously opposed naming an elementary school for the Indian woman who tried desperately to save her people while being hunted by White and Indian alike. Once Winnemucca's story was told, however, the citizens changed their minds and proudly named the school in honor of an indefatigable warrior for peace and justice.

Ignorance, prejudice, and fear still live, and it will take courageous women and men to continue the battle for equal opportunity, respect, and acceptance for all. We hope the stories of these women deepen the understanding and broaden the respect for the people who built the West.

Perhaps their contributions in the arena of service to country are best described in a quote from Colonel Henry Carrington in 1904: "Patriotism is not relegated to gender or age. It is strictly defined as one who loves, supports and defends one's country. The women who risked losing a sense of self for their homes, families and native lands have my deepest respect."

Francita Alavez, known as the "Angel of Goliad" for saving the lives of Texas prisoners of war in the "Goliad Massacre" COURTESY OF PRESIDIO LA BAHIA

CHAPTER I

Francita Alavez

Angel of Goliad

The moment Madam Alavez arrived at Copano, she began her work of intercession and performed deeds of mercy for the poor[,] suffering Texans who had fallen into the hands of the Mexican enemy.

— *PIONEER PRESS*, OCTOBER 1920

A SLIM SHADOW DARTED TOWARD THE OLD CHURCH AT THE ruined fortress of Goliad. The smell of smoke stained the night air as the figure picked a careful path through the rubble inside the fortress walls. Moonlight starkly displayed the damage caused by the retreating forces of Colonel James Fannin's command. Hundreds of Fannin's men now lay on the hard ground, prisoners of General Jose de Urrea, one of Supreme Commandant General Antonio Lopez de Santa Anna's best commanders.

Pausing in a dark corner, Francita Alavez gazed toward the southwest gate and the dull gleam of a cannon positioned to fire on anyone who might attempt a rescue of the Americans. She shivered in the warm night as the knowledge of their fate bowed her shoulders. She knew what the captives did not. They believed they would be returned to the United States as prisoners of war. Francita had seen the order sent by Santa Anna to execute all of them.

As she had at Copano Bay almost the moment she arrived in Texas, Francita vowed to save as many as she could. On the eve of Palm Sunday, March 27, 1836, she slipped into the church and began the task.

"She had heard many tales of the bad, bold, immoral Texans, but like all good souls loath to think ill of others, scarcely believed they could be as bad as painted," recounted the *Pioneer Press* in 1920. The article went on to outline what was then known about the woman who came to be called the "Angel of Goliad." Little more is known today about the young woman who worked against a dictator's orders at the risk of her own life.

According to a written recollection of schoolteacher Elena Zamora O'Shea, who learned about Francita years later through a family connection, Francita—or Panchita, as she was sometimes called—had been orphaned when young. A well-to-do family near San Luis Potosoi in Mexico raised the girl. O'Shea said that Francita was a sort of "better-class servant, of good blood and from a fine family."

O'Shea went on to describe Francita as a "pretty, attractive, loving girl chafing at her position in this family and longing to be free and to have a fling at life." Succumbing to the charms of the dashing Captain Telesforo Alavez, whom she knew to be married, Francita, "throwing all restraint aside went off with him to Texas in the campaign."

Francita's first encounter with the cruelties of war came at Copano. Mexican troops had just captured about seventy-five to eighty men after they had disembarked at the port. The Americans had come with William P. Miller from Nashville, Tennessee, to aid in the fight for liberty in Texas, then a part of Mexico. They were captured without arms and taken back to Copano.

"When she arrived at Copano with her husband, who was one of Urrea's officers," wrote Dr. Joseph H. Barnard, "Miller and his men had just been taken prisoners. They were tightly bound with cords, so as to completely stop the circulation of blood in their arms, and in this state had been left several hours when she saw them. Her heart was touched at the sight, and she immediately caused the cords to be removed and refreshments served them."

Dr. Barnard credited Francita with saving his life at Copano. He and other witnesses who survived subsequent battles called Francita's actions heroic, considering the absolute obedience expected by Santa Anna. Yet no one was sure of her true name, nor her marital status, nor the reason she defiantly continued to work against the Mexican army despite close ties to a Mexican officer.

Captain Alavez was paymaster for General Urrea. After leaving Copano, he and Francita caught up with the general, who had marched rapidly toward the key military point of Goliad and the small garrison headed by Colonel James Fannin that had been defending the old fortress.

Fannin was one of those who'd signed a broadside published six months before, in October 1835, calling for freemen of Texas to "repair to Gonzales immediately armed and equipped for war, even to the knife."

It was that kind of inflammatory rhetoric that had first brought General Santa Anna marching northward. Although Santa Anna traveled in opulent comfort, his soldiers had marched barefoot for hundreds of miles on little food, with only a small amount of ammunition, and through some of the most ferocious weather of the decade. Twice they were stopped by the infamous storms called "blue northers," where the clouds on the horizon looked navy blue and howling winds brought sleet, snow, and freezing temperatures to the balmy Southwest.

Despite a swift but exhausting advance of more than 150 miles from Matamoras to Refugio, Urrea had pressed on toward Goliad, where he expected to encounter Fannin. The rapid march was part of an overall advance of Santa Anna's generals toward key points. As more than 1,000 Mexican troops laid siege to the Alamo, Urrea caught Fannin on the open plain about a mile from cover at Coleto Creek. Fannin had made a mistake that would lead to the worst massacre of the war for independence.

Late in February, Fannin had received several urgent requests for help from the defenders of the crumbling, old mission-fort at the Alamo some ninety miles away. He had started on the road to San Antonio once, but turned back. Conflicting information on the location of the Mexican army and his lack of respect for its fighting skills led Fannin to delay a retreat from Goliad.

In a letter written a little over two weeks before the battle at Coleto, Captain Burr H. Duval described events to date to his father, William, the governor of Florida. "We are expecting an attack hourly," Duval wrote. Fannin, he said, was unpopular, "and nothing but the certainty of hard fighting—and that shortly— could have kept us together so long."

On Saturday, March 19, 1836, Fannin and his men were finally on the road in retreat from the fort. They'd buried the armament they couldn't carry and burned provisions to keep them out of the hands of the Mexican army. Later, Fannin was criticized for taking too much of the armament while leaving behind the food for his men and the fodder for the oxen pulling the heavy carts.

"Although fully determined from the necessity of the case on retreating, we were by no means disposed to run. We confidently counted on our ability to take ourselves and all our baggage in safety to Victoria," wrote Dr. Barnard in his journal.

The Battle of Coleto between Urrea's troops and Fannin's small force took place approximately six miles from Goliad. It had taken two days to get that far. Trapped by Urrea at a low point where they had stopped to allow the weary oxen to graze, Fannin's untrained volunteers inflicted heavy damage on Urrea's troops. During the first day of battle, Fannin formed the wagons, boxes, and crates into a defensive square. That night, without water for the wounded or much hope for the future, all the men voted against escaping to a forested area less than a mile distant. To escape would mean leaving the wounded behind. During the night, Urrea received reinforcements. More than 700 Mexican troops surrounded fewer than 400 Americans.

On March 20, Fannin capitulated.

Meanwhile, Captain Alavez and others had been detailed by Santa Anna to move into the abandoned fort. Francita learned of the terms of the surrender when the exhausted prisoners began to arrive. More than 200 men were marched back to the fort thinking they would be treated as prisoners of war. Urrea had dealt directly with Fannin, who agreed to surrender "subject to the disposition of the supreme government."

There was nothing Francita could do as the prisoners limped wearily forward under Mexican guns. "Nobody had yet entered the fort when, after an absence of thirty-five hours, we arrived here from the battleground," wrote Herman Ehrenberg. "The Mexicans evidently feared a concealed mine or some other scheme to cause them injury. Consequently we were the first ones to enter the desolate ruins again, but as prisoners, and were stuffed into an old church for the night. Literally stuffed, as we stood so close man to man that it was possible at the most for only one-fourth to sit down. It was well that the inner room of the church had a height of thirty-five to forty feet. If it had been lower, we would have suffocated."

Francita listened to the muffled cries for water that carried from the church. As at Copano, she could not bear the suffering of the beaten men. At eight o'clock in the morning, said Ehrenberg, six men were detailed to go to the river for water. "The first load disappeared like a single drop on a red-hot stove." The second and third days passed with only water provided—no food—for the prisoners trapped in the increasingly stifling church. They began shouting for the commanding officer and fulfillment of the terms of surrender, which they still believed meant they would be treated fairly and eventually released.

Francita was horrified to realize the prisoners believed they would be sent back to the United States. She could do little for them because determined guards stood at the side doors and several cannon threatened the entrance to the church.

Urrea had marched onward to the next battle but had sent a letter to Santa Anna asking for clemency for Fannin's troops, as he'd promised the American commander. "I issued several orders to Lt. Col. Portilla, instructing him to use the prisoners for the rebuilding of Goliad. From that time on, I decided to increase the numbers of prisoners there in the hope that their very number would save them, for I never thought that the horrible spectacle of that massacre could take place in cold blood and without immediate urgency, a deed proscribed by the laws of war and condemned by the civilization of our country," Urrea wrote in his diary. He went on to take Victoria, leaving the prisoners and the wounded behind under command of Portilla.

Meanwhile, the weather had turned hot, and the wounded had lingered on the battlefield for several days, suffering extreme thirst and pain from untreated injuries as they waited for carts to take them to the fort. As the injured troopers from Coleto were finally transported to Goliad, Francita worked feverishly with Dr. Barnard, whom she knew from Copano, and with Dr. John "Jack" Shackelford. She apparently spoke English because several survivors who did not speak Spanish repeated her words.

Santa Anna's reply to Urrea's request for clemency came back a few days later: immediate execution of the "perfidious foreigners." Another letter on March 23 to Colonel Jose Nicolas de la Portilla ordered him to carry out the execution of all prisoners.

According to the memoirs of teacher Elena Zamora O'Shea, relating the story as told years later by Francita's son, Francita "raved and railed against such commands. She begged and she pleaded for the lives of various individuals and was instrumental in saving several. She cursed the Captain [Alavez] and called him all sorts of names, *de Iscariotes hasto Luzbel.*'"

Francita was indeed beside herself. She stole into the fort with the help of some Mexican officers and concealed some of the prisoners. Drs. Barnard and Shackelford later made a special point of noting Francita's activities on behalf of the captive troops; unfortunately, she couldn't save them all. On the night of March 26, unaware that they were doomed, the captives sang "Home Sweet Home."

At sunrise, March 27, 1836, the prisoners were roused, and those who were not wounded were formed into three columns. They were lighthearted, even singing, many believing they were going home. Fifteen-year-old Benjamin Franklin Hughes recalled the moment. "We were called out and told to hurry up and get in line to march to a place of embarkation, and we got in line rather hopping and skipping for joy at the thought of soon being home. We were just about starting, when I saw quite a number of ladies standing where we had to march by."

As the columns marched out the gate, Francita watched in helpless rage. When young Hughes came near, Francita spoke to another woman, who spoke to an officer, who in turn detailed a trooper to pull Hughes from the ranks and put him with the ladies. Less than a mile from the fort, the columns, minus Hughes, were halted as the guards converged, raised their rifles, and fired at point-blank range. Most of the Goliad prisoners were killed. Some scrambled away and headed for cover as gun smoke drifted over the field. A few, a very few, managed to escape.

Hughes soon realized what Francita had done for him. ". . . in the instant of the halt the order was given to fire, and then I saw for the first time why I was taken from the ranks, and nudged up to the ladies, and immediately after some of the Mexicans came running back and began menacing me with their muskets and bayonets, as they had bayoneted all who [*sic*] were not killed outright—which they did, and even those who [*sic*] were killed were stuck through with the bayonet rather by way of sport, and such was the fate of 332 poor fellows that a few hours before were building high air castles, all to fall suddenly in a few hours with their plans."

She'd saved the boy, but she grieved for the ones whom died. Dr. Barnard saw her raging against fate. "During the time of the massacre she stood in the street, her hair floating, speaking wildly, and abusing the Mexican officers, especially Portilla. She appeared almost frantic."

Barnard credited Francita with helping conceal several prisoners inside the fort and then spiriting them away after the massacre. "When she saw Dr. Shackelford a few days after, and heard that his son was among those who [*sic*] were sacrificed, she burst into tears and exclaimed: 'Why did I not know that you had a son here? I would have saved him at all hazards.'"

Fannin, who had been wounded in the battle eight days before, was executed inside the fortress along with others unable to march to their deaths in the columns that had left the fort with a merry song. Both doctors were spared because medics were scarce among the Mexican troops. They and others were later marched out of Texas. They left behind the remains of their comrades in the form of a pile of burned bones upon the plain near Goliad.

Francita and Captain Alavez also departed, for the captain was given command of Victoria, a small town a short distance from the fortress. "As Santa Anna's army came marching into Victoria from the river west of town," said a descendant of the Quinn family of Victoria, "my grandmother looked up to find seven Americans standing in the doorway." R. L. Owens reported that reminiscences of the family indicated his grandmother warned the men they would be shot if found at the Quinn home. They turned and started away toward Texana, "but the Mexicans pursued and fired upon them, killing three or four and taking the others prisoners."

The men were taken toward the square to be executed, "but the wives of several officers threw themselves between the prisoners and the firing squad, and told the officers in charge they would have to shoot them before they could shoot these men, who had harmed no one." The men were saved.

Another survivor, Isaac Hamilton, related that he, too, had been ordered shot at Victoria, "which fate I escaped by the intercession of two Mexican Ladies [*sic*]."

Francita stayed at Victoria with Captain Alavez from March 31 until May 14. In addition to her direct intercession against executions, she reportedly aided prisoners by sending them provisions and communicating with them as she was able. Then the captain and Francita were ordered to move again, this time to Matamoros.

"After her return to Matamoros, she was unwearied in her attentions to the unfortunate Americans confined there," Dr. Barnard wrote in his journal. "She went to the city of Mexico with her husband [Alavez], who there abandoned her. She returned to Matamoros without any funds for support, but she found many warm friends among those who had heard of and witnessed her extraordinary exertions in relieving the Texas prisoners."

Barnard's account points out Francita's bravery in managing to save many of the Mexican army's enemies, given Santa Anna's orders to execute all prisoners—which even his general did not dare disobey. "It must be remembered that when she came to Texas she could have considered its people only as rebels and heretics, the two classes of all others most odious to the mind of a pious Mexican."

According to the account written about the turn of the twentieth century by Elena O'Shea, Francita had two sons, Matias and Guadalupe, by Captain Alavez while living with him in Matamoros. Elena said that Matias, as an old man working at the King Ranch in Texas, related some of the story of his mother and father. Matias claimed the founder of the ranch knew about the compassionate actions of the determined young woman who worked tirelessly and at no little risk on behalf of the prisoners marked for death. Her descendants lived and worked in Texas, and proudly traced their ancestry back to the Angel of Goliad.

"Her name deserves to be recorded in letters of gold among those angels who have from time to time been commissioned by an overruling and beneficent Power to relieve the hearts of man," summed up Dr. Barnard.

CHAPTER 2

Juana Navarro Alsbury

Alamo Survivor

We could hear the Mexican officers shouting to the men to jump over, and the men were fighting so close that we could hear them strike each other.
—ENRIQUE ESPARZA, *SAN ANTONIO DAILY EXPRESS*, 1902

THE DISTANT CADENCE OF DRUMS FROM THE NEARLY DESERTED town of San Antonio de Bexar sent a shiver of fear through Juana Navarro Alsbury. She clutched her baby son closer and strained to hear. Mexican president and General Antonio Lopez de Santa Anna, enemy of her uncle and her husband, had come when least expected, bringing thousands of men and artillery as well as a thirst for vengeance. The baby wailed at the nearby roar of exploding powder from the cannon mounted at one corner of the Alamo.

That shot signaled defiance by the Texians (Texans from the United States) and Tejanos (Texans of Mexican descent) holed up in the old mission. Juana soothed the baby and waited, holding her breath for Santa Anna's response.

It was said he had 1,500 to 6,000 troops, cavalry, and cannon at his command. Inside the crumbling fortress were several dozen women and children protected by fewer than 200 defenders. Juana's new husband, Dr. Horatio A. Alsbury, had galloped off to find volunteers to join the fight, leaving Juana and the baby behind.

Dr. Alsbury had warned that Santa Anna would come down with a heavy hand on the Tejanos and Texians who had settled in the area. Her husband's activities were known to the Mexican dictator, as were those of her father, who opposed Santa Anna's overthrow of the constitution of 1824. Her father's brother, Jose Antonio, had put his name on the Texas Declaration of Independence. If the Alamo fell under the general's onslaught, the respected name of her Spanish forebears would not protect her little family.

Juana recognized the futility of attempting to hold off the overwhelming force of hardened troops surrounding the old mission-turned-fortress. Those inside the Alamo's walls were also ill-prepared to fight Santa Anna, in part because too many people had discounted the Mexican dictator's determination. He had already killed all prisoners taken in a battle the year before and been granted by the Mexican government permission to treat as pirates all Tejanos as well as Texians found armed for battle, meaning they would be executed immediately.

The Tejanos and Texians had dismissed reports that the Mexican dictator was nearby. After all, they argued, two blue northers had recently swept through the area, their freezing winds covering the barren landscape to the south with snow. What commander would move his troops, many of them barefoot, in such conditions?

Thinking themselves relatively safe, they had celebrated the arrival on February 11, 1836, of the naturalist Davy Crockett with a fandango, a party with music and dancing and merry good spirits, despite the ominous threat said to be marching toward them. Then, on February 20, a messenger galvanized the town with news that Santa Anna's army was but twenty-five miles away. Many

The Alamo, San Antonio, Texas   LIBRARY OF CONGRESS

townspeople rushed within the walls of the old mission for protection, including Juana, her baby son, and her sister Gertrudis. The next morning, Juana's husband had galloped off to bring back reinforcements.

That afternoon Juana clutched her son in fear as she heard the drums beating a cadence for Santa Anna's march into the town square just a few hundred yards away, across the San Antonio. As the sun sank toward the horizon, defiant cannon shot thundered from the Alamo. Santa Anna's howitzers quickly fired four grenades in answer. Juana held her crying son close, praying that the saints protect him from harm. The first flurry of shots ceased. Juana began to hope.

Those hopes would be in vain.

According to Jose de la Pena, a Mexican officer in Santa Anna's regiments, a white flag was raised from behind the crumbling walls of the old fort following the first artillery volley. From inside the Alamo, James Bowie, second in command under Lieutenant Colonel William Barrett Travis, sent a message saying they wanted to discuss surrender agreements with the Mexican general.

Santa Anna was enraged. He considered the men inside the fort bandits. There could be no honorable surrender as soldiers—only death.

"When our commander in chief haughtily rejected the agreement that the enemy had proposed," de la Pena later wrote, "Travis became infuriated at the contemptible manner in which he had been treated and, expecting no honorable way of salvation, chose the path that strong souls choose in crisis, that of dying with honor, and selected the Alamo for his grave." While loyal to Mexico, de la Pena heaped criticism on Santa Anna's leadership and his brutal orders.

The red flag signifying no quarter flew over the Mexican troops as they waited. Juana understood its meaning, and the potential fate of her little family. There was nothing she could do but help prepare meals from the scanty supplies, rock her baby, and pray.

Neither the Tejanos nor the Texians inside the old fort would agree to unconditional surrender. Travis explained Santa Anna's terms to the small corps of volunteers without mincing words. "The enemy has demanded a surrender at discretion, otherwise the garrison are to be put to the sword, if the fort is taken. I have answered the demand with a cannon shot, and our flag waves proudly over the walls. *I shall never surrender or retreat.*"

The siege began that very day. Only the hope that her husband would return with reinforcements kept Juana's spirits up as she went about her daily chores.

First, Santa Anna's troops cut off the water that flowed in a ditch near the back of the church. The only other water supply came from a well in an area exposed to rifle shots from Mexican troopers surrounding the fort.

Situated as she was in the same building as the officers, near Travis and the critically ill James Bowie whom she occasionally nursed, Juana heard much that others did not, but everyone knew there was little food and only a small supply of ammunition.

That first night of the siege, according to survivor Enrique Esparza, a company of Alamo defenders went out and captured some prisoners, including one soldier who interpreted bugle calls from Santa Anna's troops. "After the first day, there was fighting every day," Esparza recalled. He was eight years old at the time, his father a Tejano defender. Santa Anna's artillery dropped cannonballs into the fort, and sharpshooters prevented access to the well.

Juana, along with the handful of other women with children at the fortress, worried that a stray bullet or a cannonball would kill her baby, or her sister Gertrudis, who shared her room. The defenders were a pitifully small force, and after more than a week any expectations that reinforcements would arrive had dimmed.

Facing the inevitable fall of the fortress, Juana slipped her baby son into a dress in the hope that Mexican troops would not harm him if they thought he was a girl. That she and her family were in grave danger could not be denied.

While he had once been close to Santa Anna, Juana's father, Jose Angel Navarro, made no secret of his support for the Mexican Constitution and his opposition to the dictatorship of General Santa Anna. The general considered her father a traitor to Mexico and had threatened him with death.

Even when they had been on good terms, Santa Anna had not been favored by the family; his courtship of one of the Navarro daughters years before had been rejected. Added to that, in 1835 her cousin Ursula had married James Bowie, well known for his support of more independence from Mexico for the Tejanos and Texians who were building a prosperous future for the region.

The political troubles of Mexico had always affected Juana's family life. The Navarros had been important in government affairs for two generations and owned ranches as well as valuable properties in the town. Juana was born late in 1812 at San Antonio de Bexar, just across the river from the Alamo. Her mother died when she was a girl, and she was raised by her aunt Josefa Navarro Veramendi at the Veramendi Palace in San Antonio.

About the age of twenty, she married Alejo Ramigio, and they had a son. Little Alejo was just an infant when his father died in the cholera epidemic of 1834. She met Dr. Horatio Alsbury when he came to confer with Bowie; he became a frequent visitor on political affairs as well as affairs of the heart as he courted Ursula.

Dr. Alsbury had been spying on Mexican forces for months and had published a broadside warning to the colonists in Texas that Santa Anna posed a serious threat. He and Juana married in 1836.

Juana prayed now that her husband would return safely with the badly needed reinforcements as well as food and medicines. She prayed for her baby and her sister and the other women and children trapped inside the walls. She spoke little English but a few years later told two American friends of her feelings and the events that led up to and included the battle and its aftermath. Mary A. Maverick and John S. Ford recounted Juana's recollections of events at the Alamo.

Juana thought it was typhoid fever that had made Bowie so ill. He refused to stay near them in case they should contract the illness, but Juana helped nurse her cousin-in-law on occasion. She described him as a handsome and gentle man who promised to care for them. Bowie and the other defenders were counting on reinforcements. Only a few men braved the battalions of Mexican troops guarding the Alamo to come to the aid of those barricaded inside.

Juana's husband had galloped off on his mission February 23. On March 1, thirty-two men from Gonzalez had arrived in a rush. Their cornmeal and coffee brought welcome relief from the diet of fresh beef supplied by the cattle corralled inside the Alamo wall. Sadly, Juana's husband was not among the new arrivals.

In a room on the northwest corner of the fort in the officers' quarters near Travis and Bowie, Juana endured the ceaseless cannonade. There was some protection from the cannonballs and rifle shots, but the situation was dire. The fort had sustained a lot of damage, and the walls had not been completely repaired.

The condition of the walls was no secret from the enemy. Mexican general Martin Perfecto Cos had fought a battle there late in 1835. Though he'd been beaten, Cos had had the walls breached in several places before he departed. Repairs were flimsy and incomplete. A ramp of dirt ascended to the east wall of the largely roofless church—that ramp proved useful to haul cannon to the top and position them for defense. Another cannon on the opposite side pointed toward Santa Anna's headquarters.

Every dawn for twelve days, Santa Anna fired into the fort. The defenders fired back. Juana and the baby were awakened each night by bugle calls from Santa Anna's troops, and the rifle and artillery fire during the day allowed no peace. The garrison was exhausted. Food was scarce. The children were fretful, the women anxious. Juana's cousin-in-law, who had tried to see that she and her son were safe, was failing rapidly. James Bowie and Juana spoke a few days before the final battle. "I never saw him again, either dead or alive," she mourned.

Then, Sunday, March 6, in the darkest hours of the night, Santa Anna secretly moved his troops into position for an assault. The moon shone dimly through clouds, hiding the movement of 1,500 to 6,000 men from the exhausted defenders inside the crumbling walls of the Alamo.

A soldier hardened by many battles in Mexico, de la Pena recalled a moment of peace just before the call to arms. "Light began to appear on the horizon, the beautiful dawn would soon let herself be seen behind her golden curtain; a bugle call to attention was the agreed signal, and we soon heard the terrible bugle call of death, which stirred our hearts, altered our expressions and aroused us all suddenly from our painful meditations."

Inside the fort, the garrison struggled awake. Juana listened in the darkness, straining to hear whether the horn meant an attack. Within minutes a volley of shots was fired, and an answering fusil-lade came from the fort. She could not see what was happening, did not know that the Mexican army had fired too soon, doing no damage to the forces inside the Alamo. Travis had shrewdly armed each man with several loaded rifles, making the return fire rapid and deadly.

The overwhelming numbers prevailed, and Santa Anna's forces breached the walls and advanced despite the withering fire of the defenders, retreating toward the old church. Juana and Gertrudis were trapped in the rooms in the northwest walls as the battle raged outside the barracks.

Travis, reported de la Pena with respect, did not take refuge as did others of the garrison. "Travis was seen to hesitate, but not about the death he would choose. He would take a few steps and stop, turning his proud face toward us to discharge his shots; he fought like a true soldier. Finally he died after having traded his life very dearly. None of his men died with greater heroism, and they all died." Bowie, who had fallen into a coma, was shot where he lay, completely unaware, on a cot in the chapel.

Juana soon understood that the "brave Texians had been over-whelmed by numbers," and hoped the Mexicans in their bloodlust would not fire on the women. Gertrudis faced the attackers first as she opened the door to find out what was happening. She ran toward Juana and the baby as the blood-spattered troopers streamed forward. The soldiers crowded into the small room shouting, "Your money or your husband!" Some broke open Juana's trunk and con-fiscated gold coins, jewelry, and even her clothing. They took the watches Travis and other officers had given her for safekeeping.

In the screaming melee inside her room, a weak and ill Texian fought his way to her side, where he was felled by bayonets of the enraged Mexican soldiers. Another man, a young Tejano, caught her arm and tried to use her as a shield, but soldiers bayoneted him and then shot repeatedly into the lifeless body at her feet. Juana clutched the terrified baby and prayed for help, a place to run, a place to hide her baby and her sister.

A Mexican officer dashed into the room and stopped the sol-diers from killing the women but forced Juana and Gertrudis out and ordered them to wait near a cannon. All around were blood and death, shots and screams, and the moans of the dying. Another Mexican officer ran up shouting a warning. "Why are you women here?"

"An officer ordered us to remain here," Juana cried out over the clamor of battle. "He would have us sent to the president."

The officer yelled that the cannon was about to be fired and they were in great danger. Cradling the terrified baby, Juana grabbed Gertrudis and threaded through the bodies to their room. Later as the sounds of battle dimmed, Juana heard her name called. She looked up to see her brother-in-law, Mexican soldier Manuel Perez, beckoning to them. Perez, her first husband's brother, had been given permission to search for them. He took them to their father's home in San Antonio. Even from there she heard gunfire that did not cease until noon.

The next day, Juana, Gertrudis, and the other women were interviewed by Santa Anna. At his elbow on the table were piles of silver coins; on the other side, piles of blankets. When each woman declared her allegiance, she was given two coins and a blanket. Contrastly, for the daughters of the Navarro family, Santa Anna had only scorn.

Three months later, Juana's husband returned with the news of the victory over Santa Anna at San Jacinto. He took Juana, little Alejo, and Gertrudis to a Navarro cattle ranch far from town. Juana's life of adventure did not end with the fall of the Alamo. A few years later, in 1842, as the struggle for Texas independence continued, Juana left home for Mexico where her husband had been captured. She followed the prisoners as they marched, stopping at Candela, where again she waited, this time for two years, until he was finally released.

Dawn at the Alamo   LIBRARY OF CONGRESS

Dr. Alsbury did not retire from his quest for independence. He joined a company of soldiers formed to fight in the Mexican War and crossed the Rio Grande. Juana was informed of his death in 1847 "somewhere between Carmargo and Saltillo."

Juana was seventy-eight when she died on July 23, 1888, at her ranch near San Antonio. Her son Alejo, whom she had protected during the fall of the Alamo, wrote her death notice.

CHAPTER 3

Susan Shelby Magoffin

Bride of the Santa Fe Trail

Rumors of invasion by Santa Anna's army kept the people in a constant state of excitement.
—*Kansas City Star, October 8, 1926*

SUSAN SHELBY MAGOFFIN GAZED AROUND THE SMALL, WHITE-plastered room in Santa Fe and wondered if she might die there. No one seemed sure where the Mexican army was or how soon a battle might commence, but there was no doubt about the danger to herself and her husband now that her brother-in-law had been taken by the Mexicans as a spy. As she had since the start of her honeymoon journey, Susan recorded the day's events in her journal:

December 1846, Tuesday 1st. *News comes in very ugly today. An Englishman from Chihuahua, direct, says that the three traders, Dr. Conley, Mr. McMannus and brother James, who went on ahead to Chihuahua have been taken prisoners, the two former lodged in the calaboza [jail] while Brother James is on trial for his life.*

Susan Shelby Magoffin, 1845 photograph from *Down the Santa Fe Trail and Into Mexico*, edited by Stella M. Drumm, published by Yale University

The messenger who brought the ominous news had gone, but the impact of the latest information from Chihuahua still reverberated like an alarm bell. The fate of everyone associated with James Magoffin hung in the balance. What if her own dear husband, Samuel, left her behind to ride to his brother's aid? They had been married less than a year, and, despite their strange honeymoon, she could not bear to be parted from the man she called *mi alma*, my soul.

She would insist on going, too, she thought. After traveling thousands of miles across wild and dangerous terrain and through the lands of unfriendly Native Americans on her prairie honeymoon, she had her courage to herself and her husband. She had survived the hazardous 1,200-mile journey despite raging storms, wild beasts, hostile tribes, outlaws, and the awful, waterless desert they had traversed a few weeks before.

⁓

Only eighteen years old in June 1846, at the start of her journey down the famous Santa Fe Trail, Susan Shelby Magoffin put her life in the hands of her Creator and of the two men she most trusted— her husband and her brother-in-law.

James and Samuel Magoffin were well known as traders in the Southwest. At least once a year, they took freight to the Mexican people and brought Mexican goods back to the United States. Two things had converged to make this trading venture different from any before it: the presence of Susan Shelby Magoffin, the first American woman to make the long, dangerous journey to New Mexico, and the secret mission carried out by her brother-in-law meant to take Santa Fe from Mexican hands.

The rebellion of Mexican and American colonists in Texas ten years earlier had gained the Texas Territory for the United

States—now the goal was New Mexico. What no one had told the eighteen-year-old bride was that her brother-in-law secretly carried critical information and instructions concerning the conflict directly from the president. Mexico had declared war, and, in May 1846, Congress had authorized President James Polk to call 50,000 volunteers into the field. The wagons piled high with trade goods were perfect cover for the secret mission.

Years later the inside story of the expedition as seen by the innocent new bride was published. "It is the story of an expedition, ostensibly a trading enterprise by two brothers, James and Samuel Magoffin, partners in the overland freighting and merchandise business, one of whom was charged with a secret diplomatic commission of important historic interest," explained the *Kansas City Star* upon the publication in 1926 of Susan Shelby Magoffin's journal.

"President Polk wanted New Mexico brought under the American Flag, but he wanted a bloodless conquest, if possible," the *Star* report noted. Senator Thomas Hart Benton of Missouri had recommended James Magoffin to Polk as "a man of sound mind, of generous temper, patriotic and rich, who spoke the Spanish language fluently, knew every man in New Mexico, his character and all the localities." So, with letters in his pocket that could brand him a spy, James set out on his secret mission. Susan was blissfully ignorant of the plan when the caravan left Missouri in June 1846.

———

"Thursday, 11th. Now the Prairie life begins!" Susan wrote in high excitement as the wagons lurched forward on that first day. She and her husband rode in a comfortable carriage from which she observed the chaotic scene. Raised in an important and politically influential Kentucky family, Susan had never even dreamed of the kind of life she would lead while traveling down the Santa Fe Trail. She carefully recorded impressions in her journal, which clearly show her early excitement:

> *It is a common circumstance for a mule, while they are hitching him in, to break away with chains and harness all on, and to run for half hour or more with two or three horsemen at his heels endeavoring to stop him, or at least keep him from running among the other stock. I saw a scamper today . . . after a fine race one of his [the mule's] pursuers succeeded in catching the bridle, when the stubborn animal refused to lead, and in defiance of all the man could do, he walked backward all the way to camp leading his capturer instead of being led.*

The young bride traveled in a train of fourteen large freight wagons, a baggage wagon, another for her maid, the carriage in which Susan and Samuel rode, and the reserve oxen and mules herded by several men. Altogether there were two women, twenty men, two hundred oxen, nine mules, a couple of horses, some chickens, and Susan's dog, Ring.

A few days into the journey, they met a trader going to Independence who related the latest news of the trail, including the fact that Natives near Pawnee Fork were giving travelers a lot of trouble. Despite that ominous warning of danger ahead, Susan was thrilled with the freedom and adventure she'd never known as a gently reared Southern belle.

Ninety-five miles into the 1,200-mile journey, she wrote glowingly of life on the prairie. "There is so much independence, so much free, uncontaminated air, which impregnates the mind, the feelings, nary every thought, with purity. I breathe free without that oppression and uneasiness felt in the gossiping circles of a settled home."

She had married trader Samuel Magoffin on November 25, 1845, at her home just south of Danville, Kentucky. Susan had older sisters, none of whom had married until well into her twenties. It was, perhaps, a little of her rebellious and adventurous spirit as well as a deep love for forty-four-year-old Samuel Magoffin that had prompted her marriage at eighteen. They'd spent the winter in Philadelphia and New York, waiting for spring and the start of the trading venture down the Santa Fe Trail.

There was also, underneath Susan's good cheer, a well-concealed fear. At a beautiful spring near Council Grove, she delighted in the scenery and the fine water, but confessed in her journal the anxiety she concealed from her husband. "I could not suppress the fear, or rather the thought of some wily savage or hungry wolf might be lurking in the thick grape vines, ready at the first advantageous moment to pounce upon my shoulders."

Susan traveled through searing summer heat, thunderstorms that rocked the plains, gale winds, torrential rains that flooded the tents and mired the wagons in mud, and lightning storms, often dealing with waterless camps with no wood for a cook fire, snakes, wolves, bison, and smaller nuisances such as mosquitoes and other insects she found particularly disagreeable.

On July 30, Susan celebrated her nineteenth birthday at Bent's Fort, the last American outpost on the Arkansas River. She was ill, as she had been off and on during the long trip. A doctor at Bent's Fort advised Samuel to take her to Europe for her health. Susan wryly pointed out that her prairie honeymoon had been undertaken for that very purpose. "I have concluded that the Plains are not very beneficial to my health so far; for I am thinner by a good many pounds than when I came out ..."

One cause may have been yellow fever or malaria; the other, undoubtedly, was pregnancy. One week after the fateful night of her birthday, Susan sadly recorded the details of her travail:

August 1846, Thursday 6th. *The mysteries of a new world have been shown to me since last Thursday! In a few short months I should have been a happy mother and made the heart of a father glad, but the ruling hand of a mighty Providence has interposed. After much agony and the severest of pains, which were relieved a little at times by medicine given by Doctor Mesure, all was over. I sunk off into a kind of lethargy into mi alma's arms. Since that time I have been in my bed till yesterday.*

As Susan labored to deliver a stillborn baby boy, she later reported that an Indian woman gave birth to "a fine, healthy baby, about the same time, *and in half an hour she went to the River and bathed herself and it*, and this she has continued each day since. Never could I have believed such a thing, if I had not been here."

The army left the fort while she remained in bed. Many soldiers were too ill to travel with the troops. Her own state of mind was revealed in a journal entry. "One must have great faith in their Creator, great reliance on his goodness, not to feel sad and uneasy to see such things passing around them—their fellow creatures snatched off in a moment without warning almost—and they themselves lying on a bed of sickness."

A few days later they left Bent's Fort. The wagons and the seventeen men needed to drive them and handle the stock were all the guard they had. "If danger were near, I should be obliged to buckle on my pistols and turn warrior myself, rather a touch above me at Amazonianism," she wryly confessed.

According to a report in *Conquest of California and New Mexico*, Susan turned warrior at least once:

> *She had it not in her nature to know fear. Through all the alarms of the camp, toils of the march, and the privations of the army, this lady was found cheerful. She was the charm of the social circle of the encampment in hours of ease, and in times of danger, brave as the bravest. Nor was her courage untried, for it happened that the carriage, getting off the line of march of the army, with only a small escort which had lagged behind, was suddenly ridden up by a squad of guerillas. Their further proceedings were instantly and timely stopped by the sight of a pair of pistols presented at them by a lovely woman.*

Susan and Samuel traveled slowly down the trail behind the army that marched a few miles ahead. Everyone expected a battle at each likely spot. Prepared for a fight at Apache Canyon, where Mexican general Manuel Armijo reportedly waited with seven thousand troops and some artillery, the Americans were informed on the eve of battle that Armijo had fled. Lieutenant William Emory described the incident in his report, *Reconnaissance in New Mexico and California*. "As we approached the ancient town of Pecos, a large, fat fellow, mounted on a mule, came toward us at full speed, and, extending his hand to the general, congratulated him on the arrival of himself and the army. He said with a roar of laughter, 'Armijo and his troops have all gone to hell, and the canyon is clear.'" So General Stephen Kearney, with about seventeen hundred men, took Santa Fe in mid-August without firing a shot. Susan and Samuel arrived in Santa Fe less than two weeks later.

She had prayed her way across the plains, past the battlegrounds where the fierce Comanche and Kiowa ruled, through the deadly

Llano Estacado, the Staked Plains, and into the comparative safety of Santa Fe, which had mysteriously been evacuated by the Mexican forces as General Kearney advanced.

Susan was somewhat reassured by the presence of American soldiers in Santa Fe. Some of the troops from the Army of the West were camped on the common across from her little adobe house. General Kearney's troopers were eager for a fight, but, down in Chihuahua, seven thousand Mexican soldiers were reportedly under arms. Contradictory stories had been coming up the trail since the wagon train's departure in July from the last American outpost at Bent's Fort, where Susan had lost her first child.

No one knew exactly what to believe, but the presence of Kearney's troops had provided a degree of comfort. Then in October, the Magoffins and other members of the band of traders departed Santa Fe, heading south after "peace" had been achieved. On the tenth of October, near Albuquerque, they learned that the Apaches were not peacefully inclined. "Report comes that Brother James has been robbed of *all* his things, carriage, mules, trunk, clothes etc[.], by the Apache Indians and escaped with his life only—how he escaped is a miracle to us. In robbing they always want the *scalps*, the principal part of the business."

As they slowly traveled south toward the Rio Grande, messages came from traders ahead of them on the trail that Mexican troops were advancing: "An express came this evening from all the traders camped below us some thirty miles, with intelligence that a large force from Chihuahua is coming to take us—that they themselves are about corralling together and sinking their wagon wheels to the hubs for a breastwork in case of attack."

Then her journal entries stop for nearly a month. Susan suffered through fever and pain for three weeks while the war effort ground to a halt. No attack came from Mexican troops, but no advance was possible, either, because the Mexican army held a vital pass. Three days into her illness, Susan's husband moved her from the tent where they had camped into the town of San Gabriel, and the army doctor treated her with quinine pills, which finally broke the fever.

On November 25, the first anniversary of her marriage, Susan reflected on the year past. "We have not been stationary any time since that event—I cannot remember one [year] as short. And it has been a happy one too. I shall be contented if all we pass together are like it."

Five days later she learned that her brother-in-law was on trial for his life, and that a large army under the direction of dreaded General Antonio Lopez de Santa Anna was marching north to retake New Mexico. Susan knew that if all the reports proved true and the scattered American forces lost the battle, she and Samuel would have to retreat. "We will certainly have to retrace our steps to Santa Fe and enter Fort Marcy for safety, for 'twill inspire this fickle people with such confidence as to his [Santa Anna's] superior and almost immortal skill that en mass they will rise on our heads and murder us without regard."

Meanwhile, Samuel's other brother, William, who had followed by a week the departure of the wagon train from Independence, had also contracted malaria and was very ill. Susan rendered what aid she could while concealing the latest news of Santa Anna's army.

On the eighteenth of December, the fate of James unknown, reports arrived that there were seven hundred Mexican dragoons in the pass and three thousand more on the way. Only nine hundred American troops were nearby. "If this force comes against them, and there is scarcely a doubt of it, what will be the consequences— 'tis painful to think of it—they must all be cut to pieces, everything seized, they march on to us here. I shall be torn from the dearest object to me on earth, perhaps both of us murdered, or at best he will be put into prison while I am sent to another without even my bible, or my poor journal to comfort me."

On the twentieth, they learned that James was still a prisoner, and they rejoiced that he had not been executed for spying. By December 29, they were in the midst of Indian attacks and learned that Mexican troops had battled Americans eighty miles down the trail. Illness struck again, and Susan nursed her family while suffering from fever herself. Then they learned of a revolutionary battle in Santa Fe, where Mexicans had attempted to take the city and execute the American leaders. Fearing to be trapped between Mexican forces, the Magoffins packed up and started north.

By January 28, 1847, they were nearing the town of Bosquecito when another alarming message arrived. "The news is that the Taos people have risen, and murdered every American citizen in Taos including the Governor [Charles Bent]. That all the troops from Albuquerque [the regulars] have been ordered to Santa Fe, leaving this portion of the territory at the mercy of the mob."

Susan prepared herself to fight. "Within our little tent we have twelve sure rounds, a double barreled shot gun, a pair of holster and one pair of belt pistols, with one Colt six barreled revolver—a formidable core for only two people to muster." With a band of hostile Indians a few miles below them on the trail and Mexican troops in the field, Susan knew the chances were good that the guns would be necessary to survival. "I wonder if I shall ever get home again? But it is all the same if I do or do not. I must look farther ahead than to earthly things."

Besides the specter of bloody battle—which luckily never occurred—the journey itself was dangerous. An eighty-mile stretch called Journada del Muerto (dead man's journey) was reached in February. They traveled across the desert at night and worried about attacks from warring Apaches by day. By March they were in El

Paso, where, in addition to everything else, a gossiping Mexican woman asked if she were never jealous of her husband, and "was quite particular to explain to me at that moment he might be off with his other Senorita."

Susan confided this tale to her journal, but refused to doubt her husband and did not tell him of the incident. News of the war was also bad, with rumors that General Zachary Taylor had been defeated at San Luis Potosi, General Wool blockaded in Monterey, a Mexican force of eight thousand capturing Colonel Doniphan's small army, and Santa Anna preparing to invade Texas. James Magoffin, they were told, had been sent south under close guard to Durango. The only good news was that he had not been executed.

Then, a few days later, while expecting the citizens of El Paso to rise up and murder them, Susan learned that all the stories were false. General Taylor had not been defeated; instead, he had been taken to Chihuahua. More American forces also had arrived at Vera Cruz. Yet, they worried about James because he had been moved, and no one knew where.

For the next five months, Susan and Samuel waited for news of James. They traveled ever southward, staying for some time in Chihuahua while the Mexican army continued its fight to preserve its territory. While staying at Saltillo, Mexico, on July 26, they heard from an Englishman just back from Chihuahua that James had been murdered in his own bedroom at dawn. On August 15, they received a letter noting that a man named Aull had been murdered, but nothing was said of James—which raised hopes he was alive. On August 20, as they were getting ready to leave Saltillo, they learned James was safe. He had spent nine months as a prisoner, expecting execution almost daily as the tide of war ebbed and flowed.

Later they learned that James escaped execution only because of his popularity with Mexican officials and officers. Some details of the incident leading to his arrest were revealed by Captain Phillip Cooke in a letter written in 1849 supporting Magoffin's efforts after the war to be paid for his services and reimbursed for expenses.

"His life was long in danger," Cooke wrote, "but I am happy to record that he dissolved all charges, prosecutions and enmities in three thousand three hundred and ninety-two bottles of Champagne wine."

Samuel and Susan returned to Kentucky late in 1847. She gave birth to another son in Lexington, who died in childhood; a daughter, Jane, was born in 1851. Susan died in October 1855, Samuel in 1888. James, who had spent nine months imprisoned in Mexico while carrying out the orders of President Polk, later was reluctantly paid by the government only about half the money that had been appropriated for the mission.

The journal of Susan Shelby Magoffin and accounts of her presence by others during that fateful year provide a level of detail and a perspective unique to early annals of western expansion. It was a journey few women would have attempted. For Susan, it was an adventure of love and a journey of understanding and insight into the people of the West.

CHAPTER 4

Frances Boyd

The Lieutenant's Wife

Surely, in no other life can women be found who are at once so brave and true.
—Mrs. Lieutenant Orsemus Bronson Boyd's view
of military wives living on the frontier,
February 1870

Miles and miles of cacti and sand stretched out before a small caravan making its way across the Arizona Territory to an army post in Prescott. Frances Anne Boyd, a petite woman barely past twenty, cast a worried glance at her husband, Orsemus, driving their wagon. The young lieutenant kept his eyes fixed on the rugged trail. Three mounted soldier escorts led the train along the dangerous path toward a canyon in the near distance. It was six o'clock in the evening and, apart from the sound of the wagon wheels bumping along the rugged terrain and the horses' hooves clopping over rocks, all was quiet.

Frances eyed the horizon before them then disappeared into the wagon. She picked up two sabers lying next to a trunk, unsheathed them, and thrust them out either side of the back of the wagon.

Frances Boyd, photograph from *Cavalry Life in Tent and Field*, by Mrs. Orsemus Boyd, published by the University of Nebraska Press

From a distance she hoped it would look like they were armed with more travelers who were ready to do battle with the Apaches. *Unless they come very close*, she thought, *the dim light will favor our deception.*

She returned to her husband's side, cradling a pistol in her lap. The strap on Orsemus' gun in his holster had been undone, and he was ready to fire his weapon as well. The riders in front of them had pulled their bayonets from their sheaths, the blades gleaming in the low-hanging sun. Frances believed the small band looked as warlike as possible. Members of the Eighth Cavalry had passed this same way a few days before and had been assaulted with bullets from some of Apache leader Geronimo's warriors. Frances and the others were relying on an appearance of strength they in nowise possessed. They knew the Natives would not attack unless they were confident of victory.

The train proceeded into the canyon. The mountain walls on either side were jagged and high. They were a treacherous color against which an Indian could hide himself and almost seem to be a part of them. Frances later wrote that their "hearts quivered with excitement and fear at the probability of an attack."

The going was slow, and, as time progressed without any hint of an ambush, the party started to relax. Then, suddenly, they heard the fearful cry of an Indian. His cry was answered by another.

Frances stared down at her baby lying at her feet. The child was bundled up in many blankets and sleeping soundly. Orsemus urged on the mule team pulling the wagon through the imposing gorge. Everyone with the party believed death was moments away. "At last, and it seemed ages," Frances later recalled, "we were out of the canyon and on open ground." The Boyds eventually met up with a large party of freighters and made their way to the northern part of the state, frazzled but unharmed. Thus was the life of a military wife on the wild frontier.

Women like Frances Boyd chose to endure the hardships of army living in order to make life for their husbands less burdensome and to help settle an untamed land. "I cast my lot with a soldier," Frances wrote in her memoirs, "where he was, was home to me."

Frances Anne was born into a well-to-do family in New York City on February 14, 1848. Her father owned a bakery; her mother was a housewife who died when Frances was quite young.

Historians record that she was a bright girl with an agile mind. She met Orsemus Boyd when she was a high school senior and he was a cadet at West Point. They were married a year later, on October 9, 1867. Orsemus had a desire to go west, and Frances had a desire to be with Orsemus.

Lieutenant Boyd was ordered to a remote outpost called Camp Halleck in the Nevada Territory. His company was to be the advance guard and protection for the proposed transcontinental railroad. Once he was settled into his quarters, he sent for Frances. Her journey over the ocean to San Francisco and across the Sierra Nevada range represented the first in an eighteen-year period during which she would follow her husband from one duty station to another. Journal entries she made while en route describe a harrowing stage ride through the California peaks:

> As long as daylight lasted we watched in amazement those wonderful mountains, which should have been called "Rocky," for they have enormous precipices and rocky elevations at many points; from the highest we gazed down into ravines at least fifteen hundred feet below, and shuddered again and again. . . . We peered into endless precipices, down which we momentarily expected to be launched, for the seeming recklessness of our driver and extreme narrowness of the roads made such a fate appear imminent.

Frances, like most military spouses, possessed an unrealistic idea of army life at the outset. She was sure that all military installations resembled the grounds at West Point. It was a notion that was quickly dispelled once she arrived at Camp Halleck. The terrain was an endless monotony of prairie, dry and dusty; a stark contrast to the lush, green fields she knew in the East. The Boyds' first home was two wall tents pitched together. The inner tent was to be used as a bedroom, and the outer one as a sitting room. Calico curtains divided the two tents; barley sacks covered the floor. Frances later remembered that the home looked much like the inside of a prison. Still, she was determined to make the best of her situation and set about making her primitive surroundings bearable.

Frances considered herself blessed to have a canvas roof over her head. Most of the soldiers did not have that luxury. The post was still being built, and until barracks were constructed the company found cover underground. Frances recalled such living conditions in her memoirs: "The men were quartered in dugouts, which, as their name implies, were holes dug in the ground, warm enough, but to my unaccustomed eyes places in which only animals should have been sheltered, so forbidding and dingy did they seem."

Like other army wives, Frances learned to adjust to her setting and worked hard to make their home, wherever it might be, comfortable. Conveniences of the day were woefully lacking. She had to learn to cook over an open flame and wash their clothes in a nearby stream instead of using a washboard and pump. Often their housekeeping goods, which always followed their arrival at the military posts, would arrive broken and chipped: "My housekeeping was simplified by absolute lack of materials. I had, as a basis of supplies, nothing but soldiers' rations, which consisted entirely of bacon, flour, beans, coffee, tea, rice, sugar, soap, and condiments. Our only luxury was dried apples, and with these I experimented in every imaginable way until toward the last my efforts to disguise them utterly failed and we returned to our simple rations."

Frances commiserated with the other wives at the post. Very few of them dared travel west with the army, and, when a new woman did arrive, they depended greatly on one another for comfort and company. New female arrivals were referred to as "sisters" or "cousins." All the women would gather together and discuss married life, children, the countryside, and travel. They would exchange recipes, clothing, and tips on how to deal with rattlesnakes, tarantulas, and scorpions.

Just as Frances had settled into life in Nevada, Orsemus was promoted and transferred to a regiment in Prescott, Arizona. It was a move she was hesitant to make. "No woman could be induced to go to Arizona," she wrote in her journal. "First, because no church was there. Second, and mainly, because many Indians were."

The trip to Camp Date Creek in Arizona was a difficult one for Frances, not only because the journey itself was arduous, over desert and rock, but because she was expecting their first child. Orsemus transported his wife to their new home via an army ambulance driven by four stubborn mules. The interior of the wagon was crowded with an array of practical items such as food and guns. Frances struggled to make herself comfortable among their tables and chairs, rifles, two pistols, and a pair of sabers. Her daughter was born en route and placed in a champagne basket between their trunks and other furniture: "A champagne basket is the proper receptacle for an infant when traveling. If with all the other hardships of that journey I had been compelled to hold baby day after day, not only would I have been far more fatigued, but she far less comfortable. Cradled in that basket, the motion of our carriage acted as a perpetual lullaby, and the little one slept soundly all the time, waking only when progress ceased."

Orsemus and Frances were forced to make a portion of the trip to Arizona without the aid of a large military escort. Frances was fearful of attack. After two close calls with Apache raiding parties, the couple arrived at Camp Date Creek in 1869. The conditions of the post were even more primitive than those at Camp Halleck, Nevada, had been. Knowing that the journey taxed every ounce of energy of her husband's mind and body, she wrote in her journal that she would "endure the crude living arrangements quietly as long as possible."

Post records show that 80 percent of the soldiers at Camp Date Creek were suffering from malaria. There were a handful of mothers with children suffering with the fever as well. Frances was petrified her daughter would get sick and that the post doctor would be forced to treat her the same way he did his other young patients: "The post doctor would plunge children with temperatures of one hundred and two or below, into a tub of cold water and hold them there until they turned blue and their teeth chattered. Heroic treatment that could not fail to wring a mother's heart."

Again Frances made the best of her circumstances, acquiring a few supplies and transforming their desert barracks into a comfortable home. She was often awakened in the night by Native drumbeats, which almost always signified the death of another soldier. Some were killed carrying the mail or patrolling the area. According to her memoirs, there was not one grave in the post cemetery whose occupant was more than twenty-three years old, and none of them had died a natural death. Frances lived in continual fear that her husband would be the next casualty.

Despite the difficulties, Frances fell in love with her Arizona home. She was content and joyful most of the time, and on a few occasions she enjoyed long rides around the post, accompanied by Orsemus. She believed the Southwest had to be one of the most beautiful spots on the face of the earth. "I could never become reconciled to localities where the eye cannot look for miles and miles beyond the spot where one stands. I dislike to think that the day will surely come when it will teem with human life and all its warring elements."

The Boyds' stay in Arizona would be a short one. Orsemus was ordered to Fort Stanton, New Mexico, ten months after they arrived at Camp Date Creek. Frances was delighted to see other women at the fort when she arrived. After being surrounded by soldiers for the duration of the trip to New Mexico, she welcomed the opportunity to converse with "sisters." With new female friends about her, she plunged into army life at the fort, setting up house, caring for her child, acting as midwife to expectant mothers, and nursing sick soldiers. It was during their time at Fort Stanton that Frances became an expectant mother again, in need of the same care she was showering on others.

Frances believed the contributions that wives made to the lives of their soldier husbands were often overlooked by military leaders. She knew that many army officers' wives made extreme sacrifices to be with their spouses. "It is notorious," she wrote, "that no provision is made for women in the army. Many indignation meetings were held (between we ladies) at which we discussed the matter, and rebelled at being considered mere camp followers. It is a recognized fact that woman's presence—as wife—alone prevents demoralizations, and army officers are always encouraged to marry for that reason."

In the spring of 1871, Frances left Fort Stanton to visit friends in New York and to await the arrival of her second child. Orsemus was able to join his wife long enough to name his newborn son, pack the family up, and move them on to yet another post in New Mexico. The couple was first stationed at Fort Union and from there dispatched to Fort Bayard, located in the remote southwestern corner of the New Mexico Territory.

Frances admired the spirit of the nomad soldiers on the American frontier. She marveled at their bravery and stamina in the face of untold danger. In addition to the pages in her memoirs devoted to treatment for sunburns, recipes for rice and hard bread, entertainment on an army post, and the modes of transportation commonly used, Frances wrote about the courageous soldier. "Though a suf-ferer all my life from army discipline, which has continually con-trolled my movements, yet, when chafing most against its restraints, I have admired the grand soldierly spirit which made nearly every officer uncomplaining forego all personal comfort for the sake of duty."

While en route to the various military posts out west, Frances described every aspect of the frontier. Traveling south through Ari-zona to Tucson, she encountered the celebrated, peaceful Indian villages of the Pimas and Maricopas. She marveled at how the Natives swarmed around the soldiers and their families with vari-ous wares for sale such as pottery and baskets. She wrote about the sites in the area and listed the San Xavier Mission as "one not to be missed when passing through." She illustrated the cacti and bushes she saw, the mounds of giant stones on the trail, and the stage sta-tions they stopped at along the way to their final destination. She emphasized again and again that they were always cautious while traveling—"for no one could tell what might happen when passing through uncharted territories."

One of the many posts at which the Boyds stopped to replen-ish their supplies was Fort Bowie in Arizona. The government's campaign against the Apache chief Geronimo was at the forefront of everyone's mind. Camp Bowie was a post nestled amid high mountains, not far from where Geronimo and his followers were thought to be encamped. The Natives often appeared on the bluffs above and fired recklessly into the outpost. Frances was worried for the safety of her husband and children, and, for the three-day stay at the camp, she could not completely rest. She was convinced the Indians were closer than she had been told.

"One evening . . . an Indian crept into the stables, and while the sentry was pacing to and fro at the farther end, mounted a fine horse standing near the entrance, and with a yell of victory horse and rider disappeared. He well knew that once mounted, pursuit could be defied."

In December 1875, Frances and her two children accompanied Orsemus to an assignment at Fort Clark, Texas. The post, located forty miles from the Rio Grande near the site of present-day Brackettville, guarded the San Antonio–El Paso road. Frances described the trip to their new post as being filled with "gorgeous, spectacular scenery." Her impression of the Rio Grande was "a beautifully, clear stream that flowed for hundreds and hundreds of miles, changing color as frequently as does the famous chameleon."

The conditions at Fort Clark were just as primitive as the previous camps to which the Boyds had been assigned. The floor of their living quarters was covered with cockroaches so large they made the ground appear black. Wood ticks had invaded the home as well, burrowing into the walls and ceiling. Frances and the other officers' wives did their best to make the quarters livable for their families. The women would share household items, decorations, and dishes with one another. The living conditions might have been crude, but the friendships forged among Frances and her "sisters" made up for the struggle of setting up house alongside every insect and reptile that happened along. Her friendships were among her most cherished possessions: "At each post I formed devoted attachments to some women, and were the love experienced for them all and their perfections to be described, a book could contain little else; for one story after another of their wifely devotion and absolute self-abnegation, carried to such an extent as to be actually heroic, is recalled."

Fort Clark saw a succession of troops coming and going on an almost constant basis. The post was located near the Mexican border, and troops were sent there to be held in readiness for any emergency—which was generally supposed to be impending war with

Mexico. Tensions ran high most of the time. Soldiers were anxious to go into battle, and, when they weren't training for combat against the Mexican army, marauding Natives, and horse thieves, they often transferred their frustrations onto those in their immediate sphere. Frances wrote about one such instance involving a suspected murderer who had been confined to the post jail. Angry troops stormed the jail, hoping to hang the accused before his trial began. The cavalry was dispatched to the scene and stopped the soldiers moments before they took the law into their own hands.

"Orsemus was called in to intercede—it was a delicate situation to handle. The sequel proved the soldiers to have been right in not trusting the law, for in Texas no crime but that of horse-stealing is considered deserving of hanging; the murderer was only imprisoned, but fortunately for himself was taken to another county."

Although Frances witnessed many stressful scenes as a military dependent, her journal entries managed to provide a balance of light and shadows within army life. The day their third child was born was a happy occasion for the family, but their joy was tempered with the news that they would have to leave their home and move into smaller quarters on post. A new officer assigned to Fort Clark had selected the Boyds' home as his new residence. "Positive experiences are tempered with minor inconveniences," she wrote. "It's the Army way."

The day Frances' second son arrived, he contracted whooping cough. The Boyds' daughter had been suffering with the illness for some time and passed it on to her baby brother after kissing him repeatedly. Within a short time, all three of the Boyd children were sick. The baby struggled the most. His coughs were violent, and at times Frances had to raise the infant to a perfectly upright position to prevent him from suffocating. It wasn't long before Frances was sick, too. The new officer would not wait until the family was well.

He demanded the Boyds move immediately regardless of the hardship: "I was at death's door with a fever when we were obliged to move. . . . Eventually each of the children caught cold, and bronchitis was added to whooping-cough [*sic*]; in consequence of which, during that and the succeeding winter, I always slept with one hand under baby's head, in order to raise him suddenly when attacked by those terrible fits of coughing."

Whatever the miseries and deprivations, Frances found the life of a soldier's wife to be "an enjoyable adventure." The men and women at army posts were quite social. They kept themselves entertained with riding and picnics, and masked balls. Frances was particularly fond of the balls and celebrated the mix of romance with the beautiful setting surrounding the post.

"One night I shall never forget. The moon shone her best and brightest on a smooth stretch of canvas, spread so as to form a splendid dancing-floor, and on trees hung with fairy lanterns, which extending as far as the eye could reach met as background the pretty little stream on whose banks lovers wandered."

From Fort Clark, Frances followed her husband to Fort Duncan, Texas, but their stay would be a short one. Not long after arriving at the run-down post, the eldest of the Boyd children came down with malaria. Texas malaria attacked its victims with such an unremitting zeal, nothing could be done until its course had been run. For three long weeks, Frances gave her eldest son and daughter round-the-clock care. Her little girl's hair fell out as a consequence of the high fever, and her son struggled to breathe. The post physician advised Frances to take her children from the territory or lose them to the sickness. Exactly ten years after she had left her home back east to begin her life as a military dependent in the West, she returned to New York.

Frances nursed her children back to health and then accompanied her husband from one outpost to another across the Midwest. Orsemus was promoted to captain and after five years returned to Texas, serving now not only as soldier but also as a lecturer on the subject of frontier living. Frances accompanied him to Fort Clark, but shortly after she was sent back to the East Coast. A band of strong-minded Apaches, led by Geronimo, was waging war, and dependents were ordered out the area. The US government was determined to capture Geronimo and his warriors, even if it took the whole army to do it.

Captain Boyd was dispatched to the Black Range in New Mexico and Frances stayed behind with the children. In New Mexico Captain Boyd was encamped with his regiment and patrolled the area in search of Apaches. It was during his stay at this temporary post that Orsemus became seriously ill, developing a violent inflammation that turned out to be incurable. He died on July 23, 1885. Frances wouldn't know of his death until several days after he had been gone. His passing took her by surprise. His letters home had ceased, but she assumed he was simply on a march and unable to write. She never imagined he was dead.

"Army wives suffer a double loss when death robs them of their husbands—the loss of both the husband and home. I was deeply attached to my life in the military and how sad it was that I must be cast adrift from all the associations of years. But such, though sorrowful in all its aspects, is the fate of army women."

In 1894, Frances turned her memoirs about her frontier life with the army into a published book. Entitled *Cavalry Life in Tent and Field*, the book is considered to be the finest in the genre. With steadfast courage and a willing spirit, Frances stood by her husband's side and brought a bit of civilization to the Wild West.

On May 2, 1926, Frances Boyd died at her home in New Jersey. She was seventy-eight. She was intensely proud of her service as an officer's wife and throughout her life fought to discredit the notion that women had no place in the frontier army: "Our presence alongside our men made their rigorous duties bearable and helped settle the frontier.... My pen glides lovingly over the paper when I begin to describe army ladies ... their sweet goodness and devotion to husbands and the cause they represented."

CHAPTER 5

Cathy Williams

Buffalo Soldier

Cathy is tall and powerfully built, black as night, masculine looking and has a very independent air both in conversation and action. Dressed in male attire she would readily pass for a man . . . she appears hard and sinewy as if her life had been one of exposure.

—*St. Louis Daily Times*, January 2, 1876

A COLD SUNRISE GREETED THE SOLDIERS STATIONED AT FORT Cummings, New Mexico, on the first day of 1868. An eager bugler sounded a call to arms, and members of the Thirty-eighth Infantry hurried out of their barracks to line up in formation, their rifles perched over their shoulders. The enlisted African-American men who made up the regiment pulled their army-issued jackets tightly around their necks in an effort to protect themselves from a bitter winter wind. Among the troops falling into place was Private William Cathay. Cathay proudly stood at attention, willing and ready to do battle with the Apaches who were raiding villages and wagon trains heading west. The determined expression the private wore was not unlike the look the other members of the outfit possessed.

The Thirty-eighth Infantry was just one of many black units known as the Buffalo Soldiers, a dedicated division of the US Army that seemed to consistently wear a determined expression. Cathay was not unique in that manner. By all appearances Private Cathay was like the other 134 men who made up Company A. What set this soldier apart from the others, however, was her gender. Cathay was a woman disguised as a man—anxious to follow orders to overtake the Chiricahua Apache warriors.

Cathay stomped her feet to warm them and allowed her eyes to scan the faces of the troops on either side. She'd been with this regiment for more than a year, and no one had learned her secret. No one knew the extremes to which she was willing to go to defend the country that had saved her from a life of slavery. Fort Cummings' commander, James N. Morgan, and his entourage approached the soldiers from the headquarters office and looked over the armed men assembled on the parade field. "The Apaches are less mobile in the dead of winter," Lieutenant Morgan announced. "In fact, this is the only time of year they are even remotely vulnerable." Private Cathay and the other soldiers hung on every word their commanding officer said. They knew this would be a dangerous mission. Many of the Buffalo Soldiers would die trying to overtake the Indians.

"The Apaches won't be expecting us to attack," Morgan added. "Using three columns, we will come at them from more than one direction and trap them." The bugle sounded again, and Private Cathay adjusted the cartridge box and gear strapped to the pack on her back. The march deep into the Apache homeland would be long and arduous. Cathay and the other Buffalo Soldiers were up to the task. She was determined to prove that she was a good soldier and worthy of the uniform she wore. As she marched out of the post with the troops toward the snowcapped mountains where the Natives had last been seen, she marched into history. Private

Cathy Williams served alongside the Buffalo Soldiers, African-American regiments raised during the Civil War. ILLUSTRATION BY CYNTHIA MARTIN, FROM AUTHOR'S PRIVATE COLLECTION

Cathay would be the first and only African-American woman to engage in active operations against the Apache.

—◦—

William Cathay was born Cathy Williams in 1842 in Independence, Missouri. Her father was a free man and her mother, Martha, was a slave on a plantation owned by a wealthy farmer by the name of William Johnson. At the age of six, Cathy began working as a house servant, performing menial tasks and assisting the Johnsons with their every need.

In 1850, the Johnsons relocated to Jefferson City, Missouri, taking with them all their possessions, including the house servants. Cathy's mother was a field hand and would be left behind. She would never see her mother again.

Cathy's position as a house servant was considered "privileged" by most slaves, but she made no distinction between those who toiled in manual labor and those who worked in the "big house." Historical records indicate that she resented her owners as much as the slaves who worked the land did. Cathy knew that in the eyes of the law she was nothing more than mere chattel owned by another human being. Like all slaves, she longed to be free. Freedom meant an opportunity to be educated, something for which Cathy ached. House servants working alongside the young woman taught her to read, but she never learned to write.

At 4:30 a.m. on April 12, 1861, Confederate gunners in Charleston Harbor fired on Fort Sumter. The Civil War had begun, and Cathy Williams' life changed forever. William Johnson passed away shortly after the first exchange of gunfire between soldiers from the North and South. Within a few months, Union troops had taken over the Jefferson City area and seized the plantation owner's property, including his slaves.

"United States soldiers took me and other colored folks with them to Little Rock," Cathy later recalled in an interview with the *St. Louis Daily Times*. "Colonel Benton of the 13th army corps was the officer that carried us off. I did not want to go."

Cathy became a free woman in the summer of 1861. It was a dream come true, but it was not without complications. She was at a loss as to what to do or where to go—she'd never known any life than that of house servant. In her former master's care, she'd had a place to sleep and food to eat. The question of how to provide for such basic necessities on her own made her freedom bittersweet. As an uneducated former slave, her job options were limited. She reluctantly accepted a paid position with the Thirteenth Army Corps as a cook. It was a job she was not eager to accept because she knew nothing about cooking. The corps commander soon realized that her culinary skills were lacking, and after a few months she was let go. She then took a job as laundress for the officers of the Eighth Indiana. She followed the unit on various campaigns throughout the South and was witness to the mass liberation of fellow slaves.

Cathy settled with the Eighth's encampment near St. Louis, Missouri. Many of the troops were suffering with dysentery and needed time away from battle to rest and recover. Although many Hoosier farm boys died from the disease, Cathy was spared even the slightest illness. She stayed with the regiment with her two twenty-five-gallon wooden tubs, soap, scrub boards and buckets, starch, laundry sticks, and other necessities.

Once the Eighth Infantry was on the mend, the company was dispatched to Pea Ridge in Arkansas. There the soldiers engaged in a skirmish that ended any Southern hopes of taking Missouri back from the Union army. Cathy's duties shifted from laundress to nurse and medical assistant. She bandaged soldiers' wounds and washed down operating tables. Five members of the Eighth were killed, their bodies torn apart in a hail of cannon and gunfire.

Cathy was deeply affected by the ravages of war. The horrors to which she was exposed included more than the deaths of young men; she also witnessed the destruction of hundreds of acres of crops and the obliteration of homes and bridges: "I saw soldiers burn lots of cotton and was at Shreveport when the rebel gunboats were captured and burned on Red River," she remembered.

One hot August afternoon, as Cathy was washing bundles of clothes, she noticed a pair of black soldiers walking toward the camp. They were wearing Union blue uniforms, tan gauntlets, and canvas hats with wide brims. Not far behind the pair marched hundreds of identically dressed black troops. The sight of the Army of the Southwest, or the Buffalo Soldiers as they would later be known, left a lasting impression upon the young woman. It sparked a desire within her to one day put on a blue uniform herself. Fighting for the Union was viewed by blacks as a holy crusade. Cathy wanted a chance to fight for the liberation of all African Americans.

As a civilian employee of the Union army, Cathy served wherever she was needed. Her work fluctuated from cook to laundress and back to cook several times. At one point she was ordered from the regiment and dispatched to Little Rock to learn how to be a mess chef. Once her training was completed, she returned to the Eighth Indiana, moving with the troops through Arkansas and Louisiana, and then up to the Atlantic Coast to the nation's capital. There the Eighth Indiana became part of the Fourth Brigade, a unit that would soon be under the command of General Phil Sheridan. Cathy was assigned to serve Sheridan and his troops. From the general's headquarters, she was exposed to many hazards and bloody battles along the Blue Ridge Mountains: "At the time

General Sheridan was making his raids in the Shenandoah Valley I was cook and washwoman for his staff."

On the morning of October 19, 1864, Cathy found her life in danger when fifteen thousand Confederates advanced on Sheridan's army. It was 5:00 a.m., and most of the thirty thousand troops were sleeping. The camp was awakened to the sound of gunfire and Rebel yells. Because the headquarters was a prime target, Cathy was caught in the turmoil of the assault. She hurried away from the scene along with a flood of other retreating Yankees. Not only did she want to escape death, but she needed to escape capture as well. If the Rebels caught her, they would surely force her back into a life of slavery. Cathy, the other camp followers, and troops made it out of the valley, vowing never to return.

The Eighth Indiana regrouped in Baltimore, Maryland, and was then dispatched to a fort in Georgia. Cathy remained with the company until the unit was mustered out of service in August 1865. After three and a half years of bitter fighting, the Civil War was finally over for Cathy Williams. She left the Eighth Indiana with a heavy heart. She had grown to love army life and could not imagine where she would go once the unit disbanded. The soldiers in Sheridan's unit recognized her plight, took pity on her, and purchased a ticket back home for her. "I was sent from Virginia to some place in Iowa and afterwards to Jefferson Barracks [in Missouri], where I remained for some time."

The locomotive transporting Williams to Missouri departed a sleepy station in Iowa, belching huge plumes of smoke into the air. Cathy stared out the window next to her seat. The car was filled with Union soldiers who had turned in their uniforms and were on their way back to their wives and families. Very few veterans had allowed themselves to contemplate until now what the future held for them once the fighting had ended. Cathy pondered the same predicament.

Overhearing two men discussing the need for troops on the western frontier planted a seed of hope in her heart. She could travel west with the army. *Laundresses and cooks are always in demand*, she thought. That notion was quickly dispelled when she heard the men add that only military personnel would be allowed to accompany the soldiers in the field.

Once Cathy reached her home state of Missouri, she quickly found work as a cook for a white family near Jefferson Barracks. While in their employ, she learned that African Americans were being enlisted in the US Regular Army. The news brought a surge of hope for her future. Her prospects as a single black woman were disappointing. As a black male, however, she could serve her country as a professional soldier. She began making plans to disguise herself and enlist. She said, "This is for the best. . . . I want to make my own living and not be dependent on relations or friends."

Transforming her look was not difficult for Cathy. Since her early days with the Eighth Indiana, she had worn men's clothing, purely out of necessity. Years of close association with soldiers helped her pattern her speaking style and mannerisms to pass as a man. She was physically fit and tall, standing over five feet, nine inches. Most women at the time were petite and frail by comparison. She was certain her height and stature would fool the brass.

On November 15, 1866, Cathy Williams marched into the recruiting depot at Jefferson Barracks and enlisted for three years of service in the US Army. She told the officer on duty that her name was William Cathy. Because she did not know how to write, the officer signed in for her, misspelling her new last name. Her age was listed as twenty-two and her occupation as cook. She requested an assignment with an infantry unit. She believed serving in such a regiment was essential to concealing her gender. All was well, but she still had to pass a medical examination by an army surgeon.

A hurried doctor looked the athletically built recruit up and down. He sized her up to be an excellent candidate for service and, with only a cursory examination, waved her through the process. Cathy, now a Buffalo Soldier, was filled with pride as she took the required oath:

I, William Cathay[,] desiring to enlist in the Army of the United States, for the term of three years do declare, that I am twenty-two years and two months of age; that I have neither wife nor child; that I have never been discharged from the United States service on account of disability or by sentence of a court-martial, or by order before the expiration of the term of enlistment; and I know of no impediment to my serving honestly and faithfully as a soldier for three years.

Private Cathay was ordered to Fort Cummings, New Mexico, to serve under the command of Captain Charles Clarke. The objective of the unit was to face the Apache force and bring the renegades to order. Cathy would be paid $13 a month to make the western frontier safe for pioneers and gold rushers. In addition to the uniform—which consisted of a dark blue blouse, lighter blue trousers, an oval US belt buckle, and brass "eagle" plates on the shoulder belt—she was issued a Springfield rifle.

Upon Cathy's arrival at Fort Cummings, she was greeted by more than two hundred African-American soldiers stationed at the post. In the short time the Buffalo Soldiers had been in existence, the unit had earned a solid reputation for being reliable and resourceful. The name *Buffalo Soldiers* was first bestowed upon them by the Cheyenne braves who saw them. The troops' curly hair reminded the Indians of the mane on a buffalo. During the post–Civil War period, these men were the roughest riders in the cavalry and hardest marchers of the infantry in the Old West. In the interview she gave to the *St. Louis Daily Times* in 1876, Cathy indicated that she was honored to be counted among them.

The hot southwestern sun felt good on Cathy's head as she marched around the outside of the fort, her eyes on the lookout for warring Apaches. Prior to her transfer to Fort Cummings, she had contracted smallpox, and her body and face had been covered with small red blisters. The illness had passed, but the chill from her stay in the cold, damp dispensary in St. Louis lingered. The New Mexico heat warmed her bones and helped shake off the memory of the sickness.

By the time Cathy had arrived at Fort Cummings, she had become an expert at hiding her gender. During her stay in the hospital, she had gone to great lengths to keep from being thoroughly examined by doctors and nurses. While marching to her new post, she drank as little water as she could so she wouldn't have to go to the bathroom often and run the risk of being found out. Cathy had two close friends stationed with her at the post who helped keep her true identity safe. They patrolled the outer perimeter of the post with her, assisting in guard duty and the protection of the fort.

During the winter of 1867, the entire post was on heightened alert. A Buffalo Soldier had been killed in the New Mexico Territory by Apaches only a month before Cathy arrived in the area. More trouble was expected. Members of the Thirty-eighth Infantry were ready for whatever lay ahead. On a few occasions, Apaches would sneak into the fort and steal horses; Cathy's job, in part, was to thwart any further thefts.

One of the most dangerous duties assigned to Cathy was that of wood detail. Members of the party sent out to collect the daily wood put their lives at risk because they were forced to travel long distances across the desert in search of fuel. These wood details were vulnerable not only because they went well beyond the safe confines of the fort but also because they consisted of only small parties of soldiers. By the fall of 1867, wood details were traveling as far as twenty-five miles west of the fort to cut trees along the Missouri River. Unless she was feeling poorly, Cathy was dedicated to fulfilling her responsibilities to the troops to the best of her ability: "I was bound to be a good soldier or die. . . . I carried my musket and did guard and other duties while in the army."

Cathy served her country across a wide expanse of the western frontier, including forts in Kansas and Colorado and throughout New Mexico and the Southwest. Yet, her service at Fort Cummings would prove to be the most dangerous of all. In January 1868, Cathy, along with the other members of the Thirty-eighth Infantry, prepared to launch an assault on the Natives who had made their stay in New Mexico so perilous.

The time had come to deal with the Apaches' attacks on army outposts. A raid on nearby Fort Bayard, a remote outpost at the base of the Santa Rita Mountains in New Mexico, had been the last straw for top military leaders in Santa Fe. During the surprise attack on the garrison, several Buffalo Soldiers were killed while horses, mules, and cattle were stolen.

Orders from the New Mexico Military District headquarters in Santa Fe instructed troops to destroy the Natives' camp, along with all adult male inhabitants who refused to surrender. The plan called for several columns of infantrymen to converge on a designated site and overtake the Natives.

The infantry marched over snowcapped mountains, through frigid desert, and across the icy Rio Grande to the area where the Apaches were encamped. The regiments were not dressed for such harsh weather conditions. They did not have heavy coats, robes, trousers, or overcoats, and they were not allowed to light fires to warm themselves because commanding officers were afraid that a blaze might betray their position. Many of the soldiers were taken ill before they reached their objective.

Finally, the Buffalo Soldiers gathered around the base of the canyon where the Apache camp was reported to be and peered down into the valley. Nothing stirred. A strange quiet filled the air. The Indians had abandoned the site, and their location was unknown. Not knowing what else to do and out of concern for the lives under his command, the company lieutenant ordered the troops to return to Fort Cummings. Tensions among the Buffalo Soldiers ran high. The troops speculated that the Natives might have slipped in behind them, planning an ambush.

By the time the Buffalo Soldiers made it back to Fort Cummings, many of them were exhausted and suffered with colds and flu. Cathy suffered from severe exposure to cold and was admitted to the post hospital. Doctors suspected she had rheumatoid arthritis brought on by the harsh weather endured in the field. The extent of her illness was not fully discovered by the army physicians because Cathy always refused examinations in which her gender could be discovered. After three days in the infirmary, she forced herself to return to duty in an effort to avoid detection.

The Thirty-eighth Infantry was transferred to Fort Bayard, which had a reputation for being one of the most dangerous posts in the West. Native unrest was on the rise at Bayard, and the unit was sent as reinforcement. Cathy was weak but wholeheartedly participated in the move and subsequent scouting and reconnaissance missions. Cathy's life, as well as the lives of the other Buffalo Soldiers, was in constant jeopardy. One of the soldiers wrote, "The Indians would come down through the pine forests close to Fort Bayard and fire into the post, and the sentinels at the haystacks were often found killed with arrows. It was unsafe to leave the post without an escort."

Cathy's health continued to decline; within a few weeks of returning to duty, she was hospitalized again. This time she was diagnosed with neuralgia. Round-the-clock attention, a proper diet, and good drinking water helped her recovery. After a month, she was on her feet again and ready to take orders from the fierce army leader she had served under in the Civil War, General Phil Sheridan. Sheridan had lost patience with the Native attacks against civilians heading west, and, in October 1868, he unleashed a merciless type of warfare on the Apaches. Sheridan would employ all the powers at his disposal to "hunt the Plains Indians down like wolves."

Private Cathay joined the hostilities, but only for a short time. Lingering poor health kept her from doing her job to the best of her ability. She was physically drained and began to tire of army life and the endless rules and regulations. The problem of racism within the army as a whole contributed to her change in attitude as well: "I performed all the duties expected of a soldier. . . . I was never put in the guard house, no bayonet was ever put to my back. . . . Finally I got tired and wanted to get off."

Historians speculate that Cathy was tired not only of military life, but also of living a lie. The endless masquerade, no doubt, took its toll on her emotional health. After nearly two years of service, she marched over to the hospital determined to end the charade. The post surgeon met her as she walked into the building.

"I got tired. . . . I played sick, complained of pains in my side, and rheumatism in my knees." Cathy made no attempt to hide her gender on her final visit to the post infirmary. During a routine exam, her gender was finally revealed. The discovery would have swift and immediate repercussions.

"I got my discharge. The men all wanted to get rid of me after they found out I was a woman. Some of them acted real bad to me."

⌁

In October 1868, Cathy Williams became a civilian again. She resumed the garb of a woman and traveled to Fort Union, New Mexico. For two years she worked as a cook for a colonel and then moved to Pueblo, Colorado, where she was employed as a laundress for a businessman and his family. There she was introduced to a local miner who asked her to be his wife.

"I got married . . . but my husband was no account. He stole my watch and chain, a hundred dollars in money and my team of horses and wagon. I had him arrested and put in jail." After her divorce, she left Pueblo and moved to Trinidad, Colorado. She liked the town and the people and decided to make the growing settlement her home. She continued working as a laundress and periodically served as a seamstress and a nurse. Cathy hoped to obtain a land grant from the Homestead Act of 1862. She had plans to take her land near the depot after the railroad came through. "I expect to get rich," she told the *St. Louis Daily Times*. Her dream was partially realized in Colfax County, New Mexico, when she relocated to the area and became a businesswoman, running a boardinghouse.

A St. Louis reporter, who had heard rumors that Cathy served with the Buffalo Soldiers, sought her out for an interview. After his article was published, Cathy Williams became the focus of local curiosity. No one suspected this quiet, hardworking African-American woman had had such an adventurous past.

After she had saved enough money, Cathy returned to Trinidad, where she purchased a farm. She grew vegetables and flowers and in so doing broke another barrier: This former slave woman owned the land she worked. Cathy's long-standing health problems resurfaced again in late 1890, and she had to be hospitalized. Unable to make a living for herself, she filed for military disability, hoping to get some help with her expenses. An army doctor was sent to Trinidad to examine the ailing ex-soldier and judged her to be fit. "Apart from a few amputated toes," his report read, "I do not find she is suffering from rheumatism, neuralgia or any other illness that might be [attributed] to her service." Her disability pension was denied. Attorneys worked on her behalf, but to no avail. Her case was repeatedly denied.

Military historians speculate that Cathy Williams died sometime in the early spring of 1892. Rheumatism had crippled the former army private, who also had developed diabetes. According to historical records, complications from diabetes most likely caused her death.

No record can be found in the small town of Trinidad of the final burial place of Cathy Williams. She was more than likely buried in an unmarked grave in the Black cemetery. She was fifty when she died.

CHAPTER 6

Charley Hatfield

Gallant Rebel

*Always armed with a revolver or two in her belt and a long
sheath-knife in her bootleg, she seemed perfectly able to protect
herself in any emergency.*
—George West, publisher of the *Colorado Transcript*, January 14, 1885

Music from an out-of-tune piano spilled out of Schell's
Saloon in St. Louis and bounced off the buildings up and down
Vine Street. A hot breeze pushed past Charley Hatfield, an overgrown cowboy with a cherub's face, as he sauntered up to the
swinging doors of the weather-beaten bar and gazed inside. It
was the summer of 1854, and every saloon in town was filled with
thirsty, ambitious people en route to the gold fields in California. It
wasn't Charley's love of gold that was driving him west, however;
it was something more primal. He had been driven to this place
by revenge.

Charley surveyed the scene before him. His eyes fixed on a
swarthy, careworn man sitting at a poker table in the back of the
room. There was no doubt in his mind that he had found the man

he'd been looking for—a character named Jamieson. Charley had memorized his enemy's face; the features had been burned indelibly into his mind.

Wandering over to the bar, Charley ordered a beer from a scraggly bartender. In the mirror behind the dusty counter, he watched Jamieson deal a hand. Ever so slowly Charley's hand sought the butt of his revolver cradled in the holster on his hip. He toyed with the notion of putting a bullet into Jamieson's head right then. "It would be too cowardly," Charley mumbled to himself as the bartender slid his drink in front of him. "Before I send him to the unknown, I want him to know why," he added as he swallowed a big gulp.

Charley picked up his beer and walked closer to the table where Jamieson was sitting. He wanted to study the face of the man who had tormented his soul for more than five years. While he watched Jamieson win hand after hand, his mind mulled over the reason he was here. He remembered how Jamieson had shot the one person he loved more than anything. He remembered how happy his life had been, right up to the hour Jamieson had crossed his path. Charley pulled his hat low over his eyes in an attempt to hide the strong emotions etched into his face. Jamieson, completely unaware of what lay ahead of him, laughed a hearty laugh while raking his winnings into a pile.

A giant clock over the bar chimed midnight, and the card game suspended. Jamieson filled his pockets with his money, tipped his hat to the gamblers around him, and headed out the back door. Charley waited for a moment then exited the same door Jamieson used. It deposited the men into an alleyway behind the saloon. A full moon cast long shadows over the pair. Charley called out to Jamieson. The man stopped walking and cast a glance back at Charley.

"I want to talk to you," Charley blurted out.

Jamieson studied the young man's face but didn't recognize him. "With me?" he asked.

Charley nodded. "I've followed you for that purpose, and I may truly say I'd have followed you a good deal farther to speak with you!"

Jamieson half smiled, suspecting nothing sinister. "What can I do for you?" he replied.

Charley took a few steps toward the man, his heart pounding in his chest. "You've done a good deal for me already, and I've come to thank you for it," he snapped.

Jamieson scratched his head. He searched Charley's face again, hoping something would come to him, but nothing did. "You're mistaken, I reckon—I don't know you."

Jamieson spun on his heels and started down the alleyway again. "I think you must be drunk, friend," he added. "Suppose we go somewhere and grab a beer? Perhaps I shall then know you as well as you know me—that is, if we can find anyplace open at this time of night."

Charley choked back the rage he was feeling. He clenched his fist at his side. "How about I refresh your memory right here?" he asked gravely.

Jamieson stared hard. "Go ahead," he said.

Charley stepped out of the shadows, his face completely exposed in the moonlight. He wanted Jamieson to get a good look at him. "A few years ago there lived in a city on the Mississippi a happy family," Charley began, "consisting of a husband, wife, and two children. They were in comfortable circumstances. He was a kind, affable, affectionate, loving husband, and an indulgent father. The young mother was trusting and happy in her maternal duties and the love of her husband." Charley paused for a moment. He could tell Jamieson was trying to remember.

Charley Hatfield (right), 1896   COURTESY OF THE PROPHET FAMILY

"What's all that got to do with me?" Jamieson finally responded.

Charley took a step closer to the bewildered man. "Everything," he said. "In one moment, the wife was made a widow, the children orphans, the husband hurried to an early grave."

A look of inquiring horror filled Jamieson's face. "What of all that?" he asked.

"I'll tell you," Charley continued. "The wife, hurled from happiness so high into misery so profound, swore to be avenged upon him who had drawn her into this ruin. For this she foreswore her sex, she mingled with rough men, and sank her nature in the depths to which associations with rude characters plunged her. Through all these she persistently pursued the object of her mission. Her search lasted long, weary years, but she followed it until at length she was rewarded. This night she followed him to a gambling hall, and when he left she met him, harrowed up his guilty soul with a narration of her wrongs, and then ..." Charley removed her hat and brushed her hand through her short, blond hair.

Jamieson looked on; his eyes widened. Hidden under the denim and leather garb was indeed a woman. At one time she was probably a lovely girl, but now she looked as if she'd endured many agonizing, tortured days. Her skin was lusterless; lines of fatigue pulled deeply around her mouth and eyes. Jamieson studied her expression carefully.

Charley inched her hand up toward her gun while continuing with her story. "She did as I do now," she announced. "Drew her revolver, cocked it, and sent his black soul to the devil who gave it to him."

In one fast, clean move, Charley reached for her gun and fired at the man in front of her. Jamieson sprang backward, drawing his own revolver in the process. A pair of shots rang out, and Charley dropped hard to the ground. One of the bullets from Jamieson's gun had found her thigh. She raised herself up a bit and fired off another round. Jamieson yelled with pain as he hurried out of the alleyway. In the brightness of the moon, she could see his left arm dangling at his side and noticed the blood pouring from the wound. She had hit him twice in the shoulder.

Jamieson jumped onto his horse that was tied at the end of the alley and sped off into the night. Charley squeezed off one more shot before falling face-first into the dirt and fainting.

——— ———

According to a report from the *Colorado Transcript*, when Charley Hatfield was born in 1837, her mother gave her the name of Charlotte. Her friends and family called her Charley. The circumstances surrounding the infant's birth were just as controversial as the life she would later lead.

Charlotte was the product of an affair between two lovesick people who had pledged themselves to each other for an eternity. They were eager to marry, but their nuptials were postponed by a death in the family. Charlotte's father left his betrothed in Louisiana, where they lived, to settle the estate he had inherited in Kentucky. For a while the pair continued their romance through the mail. When the letters stopped coming, Charlotte's mother assumed the young man had had a change of heart, and she married another. When her fiancé eventually returned and learned that his beloved had wed, he was heartbroken. After a brief encounter, the two separated. He left her to her husband and returned to France, where he had been born. He never knew he had a daughter.

Ashamed and financially unable to care for her child, Charlotte's mother sent her to live with her uncle in New Orleans. Charlotte was raised believing that her parents had died and that her mother was her aunt. It wasn't until Charlotte was fifteen that she learned the truth. Looking back over her childhood, she remembered how her aunt's eyes would fill with tears and her voice would choke back sobs when they were together. She later recalled, "My remembrances of the place and its people are misty—all about it seem more like something I once saw in a dream, but whose characters time has effaced."

At the age of twelve, Charley left the boarding school where her uncle had sent her and married a riverboat pilot. She wrote that he was a "noble fellow and well repaid the sacrifice made for him." When her uncle heard about the elopement, he disowned her. She was so much in love with her husband that she dismissed her uncle's reaction outright. "I did not regret getting married. . . . I was happy beyond my most sanguine expectations," she would later recall.

By the couple's third year of marriage, they had two children, a boy and girl. Charlotte was elated with her life. "I believe that now the circle of my enjoyment was complete. My husband, though much absent, was unremitting in his love—I had two, bright, healthy children, what more could a woman ask?"

Charley wouldn't know happiness for long. Three months after the birth of her daughter, news came that her husband had been killed. "A man named Jamieson . . . ," the messenger reluctantly began. "They argued over an old grudge and then Jamieson shot your husband." Charley went through the next month of her life in a fog, devastated by her loss. After paying for her husband's burial and settling his outstanding accounts, she had very little money left to support her children. Being a woman and untrained for any profession, she found acquiring reputable work impossible. She decided to disguise herself as a man to gain employment. "It was my only resort from starvation or worse," she later wrote in her autobiography. She placed her children in the care of the Sisters of Charity and set about to make a new life for herself, vowing all along to find Jamieson and kill him for depriving her son and daughter of their parents.

Charley was convincing as a man. She cut her hair to the proper length and donned a suit. Her appearance did not differ materially from that of any boy of fifteen or sixteen. She found a job as a cabin boy on a steamer and rose through the ranks to eventually become a pantry man. Once a month, she would change back into her dresses and petticoats and visit her children. Her absence from them was torturous; she later recalled in her autobiography: "My children would haunt my dreams and play about me in my waking hours—the separation seemed intolerable, and for the first month an eternity."

Charley's work would take her up and down the rivers of the Midwest. She kept a keen eye out for Jamieson at every port. Her first confrontation with Jamieson, outside Schell's Saloon, had left her with a broken thigh. It would take six months for her to heal. Once she was up and around, she decided to head for the "Land of Gold."

In the spring of 1855, she joined a wagon train as a bushwhacker and headed for California—the only woman in a party of sixty men. Charley recorded her overland route with great detail. Her diary included such trail markers as Court House, Chimney Rock, Scotts Bluff, Mormon Ferry, and Independence Rock. Her journal would later be used to guide several wagon trains bound for California and Oregon.

The way west was full of every kind of danger and privation. Charley lost 110 head of cattle upon reaching the alkali waters around Salt Lake. Despite her best efforts, the thirsty animals couldn't be stopped from drinking the deadly water. Once the tired and weary wagon train, along with the remaining livestock, made it to the Humboldt River, they were attacked by a band of Snake Indians. Charley managed to shoot one Native and stab another before being severely wounded in the arm.

With her arm in a sling, Charley led her battered wagon train on to California. All attempts at finding gold were a bust for her, however; so she sought other business opportunities—owning and operating a saloon, running a pack mule service, and buying into a cattle ranch. The cattle ranch was the most successful venture, turning a $30,000 profit in a short time.

In 1859, Charley relocated to Colorado and began panning for gold around Pikes Peak. Again, she had no luck in finding the glittery substance and decided to abandon all notion of finding the mother lode in favor of opening a bakery and saloon. She made money rapidly, but a bout of mountain fever forced her to give up the business and move to Denver. While she was there she became preoccupied with the news of civil war breaking out. She felt compelled to join the fight against slavery and was sure her disguise would afford her the opportunity to do so.

In September 1862, she enlisted and served with both the Second Colorado Cavalry and the First Colorado Battery. She was assigned to General Samuel R. Curtis' regiment at Keokuk, Iowa, and because of her good penmanship was detailed to headquarters as a clerk. When the Battle of Westport in Missouri broke out, Charley acted as a courier, carrying orders and messages all over the command area. Often she had to travel to the front. Her commanders praised her for her "coolness and bravery."

The first day of the conflict left the Union army with a number of casualties. General Curtis shared with Charley his desire to ascertain the enemy's battle plans for advancing. Upon hearing this, Charley conceived a way to get into the Rebels' camp and find out their next move. She borrowed a dress, sunbonnet, and other female fixings from one of the laundry women and transformed herself back into the lady she once was. Armed with a basket of eggs, she snuck across enemy lines and into the Southerners' camp.

Her modest, unassuming, Missouri country-girl act worked well. She was able to gain access to Confederate general Joseph O. Shelby's staff and found out that the Rebels had a fix on the Union army's cannon company. While eavesdropping on several other conversations around the campsite, Charley learned everything the Rebels knew about the Yankees' positions. Just as she was about to be escorted out of the area, a courier rode up fast and presented a dispatch to the general. Shelby read the message, then jumped to his feet and began barking orders to the troops around him. "Boys," he shouted, "I want the picket along the river doubled! Be quick and quiet! I want twenty of our best men in their saddles quick as lightning."

The soldiers around the camp leapt into action. There was so much activity that no one took notice of Charley as she snuck into the woods. She watched the disposition of the troops from behind a tree. As the general mounted his horse, he dropped the dispatch on the ground. Charley waited for the camp to clear, then grabbed the message and disappeared into the timber.

Charley made her way down the river, through the dense forest, and back to her regiment without notice. She presented General Curtis with the dispatch, and he immediately moved his men into position. The message revealed a surprise attack the Rebel army was planning to make on Curtis's company. Curtis had enough time to realign his troops just before they were fired upon.

Charley was recognized for "bravery displayed in the execution of her perilous trust." She accepted the praise modestly and with many expressions of thanks to the general for his confidence in her "patriotism and worth to the service."

Charley Hatfield traveled throughout the West, passing by such trail markers as Scotts Bluff, Independence Rock, and Chimney Rock. LIBRARY OF CONGRESS

The fighting along the Missouri River was far from over, however. The Battle of Westport resulted in heavy losses for both sides. Charley was among the injured. Confederate soldiers found her on the ground alongside her dead horse. She had a gunshot wound in her leg and a saber cut in her shoulder. She was taken prisoner by the Rebels and removed to a nearby hospital.

Army doctor Jesse Terry removed the coat from Charley's unconscious form. While inspecting the cut on her shoulder, he made the startling discovery that Charley was a woman. He decided to keep the news to himself. He dressed her wound and replaced her jacket, never saying a word to anyone.

When Charley regained consciousness, she anxiously sought out the doctor who had nursed her back to health. Terry could tell she was concerned about what he discovered about her, and he quickly put her mind at ease. "Your secret is safe with me until you are able to tell me your story," he told her. "There is not time now and this is no place to hear it."

During an exchange of wounded prisoners, Charley was freed and transported back to her regiment. While she was recuperating, she learned that General Curtis had recommended her for a promotion. She was soon upgraded to first lieutenant and served out the rest of the war with her unit. Dr. Terry kept his word and never told anyone of Charley's true identity.

Charley continued with her life dressed in male attire. She never failed to provide for her children and never fully abandoned her search for Jamieson. It was while she was on an excursion three miles from Denver City that she came in contact with the man again.

Charley and Jamieson rode toward each other on a narrow road through a mountain pass. He was riding a mule, and from a distance Charley thought there was something familiar about his countenance. As they neared each other, she began to realize that it was Jamieson. At roughly the same time, he recognized her, too. He went for his revolver, but Charley was a second too quick for him.

Charley sent a bullet Jamieson's way, and he tumbled off his mule. A bullet from his gun whistled past Charley's head, just missing her. She leveled her revolver at him as he tried to pull himself to his feet. Two more rounds sailed into his body, and he fell down again. He wasn't dead, but Charley was determined to change that. Just as she removed a second revolver from her holster, two hunters came upon the dispute. The hunters stopped the gunplay, constructed crude irons, and hauled Jamieson to Denver. Charley followed along behind them, cursing the murderer of her husband the whole way.

Jamieson was taken to a boardinghouse and examined by a physician. Three bullets were removed from his body, but none of the wounds proved fatal. Within a few weeks, he was back on his feet and telling anyone who would listen the whole story of Charley's past life. He explained why she was after him and absolved her of blame. He left town and headed for New Orleans.

When word of Charley's true identity made the papers, she became famous. Her efforts during the Civil War were now made all the more astounding in light of the truth of her gender. Charley sought refuge from her newfound popularity back in the mountains around Denver. There she married a bartender by the name of H. L. Guerin. The two ran a saloon and a boardinghouse before selling both businesses and mining for gold. The couple had two children together. Charley penned her autobiography in 1861; subsequent details about her life were published in the *Colorado Transcript* newspaper twenty-four years later by a reporter who claimed to have known Charley and served with her in the cavalry.

Some historians believe there were more than one "Charley Hatfield," and that the stories of their lives have intertwined over the years to become one. Still others insist that there was only one person by that name—a daring woman unafraid to fight for liberty, for herself, and for the nation. Historical records show that she eventually moved to St. Joseph, Missouri, and lived out her days surrounded by her loving family.

CHAPTER 7

Winema

Woman Chief

*Of the several characters developed by the Modoc Indian War of
1873, none stands out with more claim to an honorable place in
history than Wi-ne-ma, the woman-chief.*
—ALFRED BENJAMIN MEACHAM, MEMBER OF THE
INDIAN PEACE COMMISSION, 1876

A LONE NATIVE AMERICAN WOMAN CAUTIOUSLY LED HER
chestnut mare through the bluffs around Klamath Lake, an inland
sea twenty miles north of the line dividing California and Oregon.
The rider was Mrs. Frank "Tobey" Riddle. She belonged to the
Modoc tribe that settled in the area; they called her Winema. She
was known among her family and friends as one who possessed
great courage and could not be intimidated by danger. She pressed
past the jagged rocks lining the transparent water, praying to the
great god Ka-moo-kum-chux to give her abundant courage in the
face of the certain danger that she was about to encounter.

Winema was a mediator between the Modoc people, other
Indian tribes in the area, and the US Army. With her skills, she
was able to negotiate treaties that kept the land of her ancestors

in peace. Whenever that peace was threatened, her job was to set things straight. She was on her way now to do just that—riding into hostile Modoc territory to persuade the chief to surrender to the cavalry.

Chief Keintpoos, or Captain Jack (a name given to him by the settlers because of his liking for brass buttons and military medals on his coat), was Winema's cousin. In 1864, the US government forced his people from their land onto a reservation in Oregon. Conditions on the reservation were intolerable for the Modoc people. They were forced to share the land with Klamath Indians of the region. The Modoc and the Klamath tribes did not get along. The latter particularly hated the Modoc people because they had long been defeated by them in battle. Now suddenly their old enemies were moved into their midst. The Modoc Indians struggled to live in this hostile environment for three years. Modoc leaders appealed to the US government to separate the tribes, but officials refused to correct the problem. In 1869, Captain Jack defied the laws of the white man and led his tribe off the reservation and back into the area where their forefathers had first lived.

The cavalry and frustrated members of the Indian Peace Council wanted to use force to bring Captain Jack and his followers back to the reservation. Winema persuaded them instead to give her a chance to talk with the chief. "No peace can be made as long as soldiers are near," she told them. "Let me speak with my cousin and see what can be done without war."

As Winema made her way around the jagged sides of the mountains, she thought of her son. Before she'd left on her journey, she'd held the infant in her arms and kissed his lips. Although she was traveling under a flag of truce, she considered the possibility of being seen as a traitor by her people and being struck down before she could plead her case. She shuddered a moment at the thought, then, with a set face, spurred her horse forward. *I will see my little boy again*, she promised herself.

When Winema reached the Modoc camp, Captain Jack's men gathered around her. A dozen pistols were drawn upon her as she dismounted. She eyed the angry tribesmen as they slowly approached her. Then, walking backward until she stood upon a rock above the mob, she clasped her right hand upon her own pistol, and with the other on her heart she shouted aloud, "I am a Modoc myself. I am here to talk peace. Shoot me if you dare, but I will never betray you." Her bravery in the face of such difficulty won the admiration of her people, and, instantly, a dozen pistols were drawn in her defense.

—⁓—

Winema was born near the Link River in Oregon. Her mother died in childbirth. She was raised by her father, older sister, and brother. From a very early age, she had displayed abilities usually relegated only to adults. While canoeing with friends on a lake, for instance, the boat was drawn into a strong current. The canoe was in danger of being plunged through a rocky chute. Anxious parents on the shore watched in horror as their children were rushed toward certain death. Undaunted, Winema stood up and steered the canoe around the huge boulders until it reached the calm surface of the lower lake. It was here that she was called for the first time Kaitch-ko-na Winema, the little woman chief.

Winema was regarded by her people as an extraordinary child. The elders in the tribe told her stories of her heritage; her father took her on grizzly bear hunts and taught her Modoc traditions. While she was still a girl, she encountered a white settler—an experience that fired her heart to learn all she could about the white man's history and how it differed from her own.

Winema, celebrated Modoc Indian who saved Albert Meacham's life in 1873, sits next to her son, Charka. LIBRARY OF CONGRESS

This particular white man had been on his way to Oregon when he got separated from his wagon train and became lost. When Winema and her father happened upon the man, he was alone and starving. They helped him to their village and nursed him back to health. While recuperating, he shared stories with Winema about the great cities and towns in the East and of his wonderful civilization and its achievements. Winema was fascinated. She shared the stories of this "new people" with her friend U-le-ta. It did not hold the same interest for him. He tried to convince her that such knowledge was worthless, but Winema could not be persuaded. Her desire to know more of the white man's heritage only grew stronger.

Occasionally, members of the Modoc tribe would visit the miners in and around Yreka, California. It was on one of those visits that Winema first met Frank Riddle, the man who would become her husband. Frank was a prospector, bent on finding the mother lode. He had left his betrothed in Kentucky with the promise that he would return with his weight in gold and marry her on the spot. He never imagined a Native woman would steal his heart. The two were wed a few short weeks after meeting.

Winema quickly settled into her role as a miner's wife. She cooked and cleaned and was known by most in the camp as "a first-rate housekeeper." The couple would visit her people in the dry season. Frank would hunt and fish with her father and brother and was known as the one who "won over the hearts of the Modoc tribe."

Frank and Winema made their home on a ranch not far from Yreka, but there was no peace for the two or the land. Several tribes in the southern portion of Oregon were at war. Many bloody battles were being fought near the Riddles' homestead and at times in the streets of town. Driven by the unrest in the area and saddened by the Natives' inability to get along, Winema took it upon herself to act as mediator among the tribes and, at times, between her own race and the white man. She organized a treaty council and enlisted members of the fighting bands to participate in peace talks. An agreement was reached among all parties, and for a time bloodshed was avoided. Winema was known by all in the territory as "the one who could make peace, and who always calmed the threatening tempest arising from contact of races."

Less than a year after a peace treaty was agreed upon, the US government defied the terms by refusing to recognize Captain Jack as chief of the Modoc people. The government had also violated the treaty, as noted, by forcing members of the Klamath tribe to share reservation land with the Modocs. Believing the agreement between the Modoc people and the United States broken, Captain Jack felt justified in leaving the reservation.

A peace commission consisting of three government officials was dispatched to Yreka. It comprised General Edward Canby, Methodist preacher Eleasar Thomas, and a onetime superintendent of the Modoc Reservation, Albert Meacham. Meacham knew that Winema and Captain Jack were related and asked her for help in persuading the chief to return to the reservation. Winema agreed, but Captain Jack would not relent. Finally, in 1873, four years after the Modoc chief led his people off their designated land and after seeing his cousin's courage as she faced his warriors on the rock, he gave in to Winema's request.

The first meeting between Captain Jack and the government officials took place on a cold winter day. Strong winds blew snow against the sides of the council tent. The chill in the air was from more than the weather. Captain Jack did not trust the commission and wore his mistrust like a badge of honor. Winema took her place beside her cousin, across from Canby, Thomas, and Meacham. She rendered their English into Modoc, and, after several tense moments, the question on the commission's mind was asked.

Winema studied the chief's face, waiting for him to respond. "Will I go back to the reservation?" he repeated dully. "All right," he went on. "Provided my people be given Modoc Point on the Klamath Reservation for our home." Meacham and the others agreed. They celebrated the end of the conflict by cheering and patting one another on the backs. Captain Jack took offense at the demonstration and jumped to his feet. His braves drew their pistols on the unsuspecting commission. Winema reacted quickly, placing herself between the government officials and the Indians.

"Wait, wait, until I talk!" she shouted. "Don't shoot. Hear me!" She placed her hand on the drawn revolvers and talked the braves into lowering their weapons. She begged the commission to be patient. "My cousin has a good heart," she insisted. Winema took command of the talks. She enthralled both parties with her speech about peace. The meeting ended with the Modoc chief and all his people returning to the reservation.

Within a few short weeks, however, trouble on the reservation escalated again. The lives of Captain Jack and his people were constantly being threatened by members of the Klamath tribe, it seemed, and the US government was not providing the Modocs with protection. Captain Jack and followers left the reservation for a second time; no amount of talking from members of the peace commission would entice them to change their minds.

Major Jackson of the US cavalry was organizing his troops for an attack against Captain Jack and his braves when Winema made a final appeal for a nonviolent resolution. "If you take these Modoc by force," she told the major, "no peace could ever be made." Jackson waited until two of his divisions had surrounded Captain Jack's camp before it was agreed that another set of peace talks was in order. Winema was dispatched to the Modoc camp to make the arrangements for the meeting.

Captain Jack did not welcome his cousin with the same warmth as he had in the past. He scarcely made a move to protect her when the braves greeted her with loaded weapons. He was furious about the government's broken promises and, at first, would not listen to Winema's request for another meeting with the government officials. After several hours of taunting her with the breaches of the contract for peace negotiations, he agreed to meet with the commission the following day. Something in his countenance made Winema suspicious of his motives. She left the camp feeling uneasy about what lay ahead.

On April 11, 1873, General Canby, the Reverend Eleasar Thomas, and Albert Meacham made their way to the site where they were to meet with Captain Jack. Winema rode with them. The peace commission had agreed to come to the meeting unarmed, a notion with which she strongly disagreed. She tried to convince Canby that they should be cautious. "Captain Jack and his braves do not trust any longer," she told the general. "There could be trouble." General Canby suggested that Winema was wrong and only frightened by her experience with Captain Jack the day before.

The tension inside the tent where the talks were to be held was thick. The peace commission sat on one side, Captain Jack and his men on the other. Winema placed herself between them all. Captain Jack was one of the first to speak. "Will you remove the soldiers from our land and give my people a home in the country?" he asked. "If the soldiers should be removed, the phantom of death would pass as a dream," he continued. "If they should not be withdrawn, the phantom must soon become a terrible reality."

The three members of the peace commission fearfully looked on. With dignity befitting a soldier of his standing, General Canby pronounced firmly, "I cannot withdraw the soldiers."

Winema watched the anger intensify in Captain Jack's eyes as she interpreted Canby's response. In one fast instant, Captain Jack drew a pistol and shot General Canby in the face. One of the Modoc braves fired a shot at Thomas, hitting him in the hand. He jumped to his feet and started out of the tent. Another Indian shot him in the back of the head. By the time the violence turned to Albert Meacham, Winema had thrown herself in front of him. With her arms outstretched, she pleaded for his life. A brave pushed her out the way and put a bullet through Meacham's left eye, blinding him. Winema laid down on top of Meacham, shouting, "Don't shoot anymore!"

Captain Jack stood up and stared down at his cousin. "Take care of your white brother," he told her. The Indians rushed out of the tent, leapt onto their horses, and rode off.

Winema wiped the blood from Meacham's face and straightened his limbs. She believed he was dead. She looked around at the bodies of Thomas and Canby. They had been scalped and stripped of their clothing. Tears filled her eyes, and she dropped to her knees, crying.

Winema quickly regained her composure and rushed out of the tent. Looking south, she saw her cousin and his comrades on horseback racing away from the scene. The sun reflected off the brass buttons of General Canby's uniform, which Captain Jack was wearing. Looking north, Winema caught sight of the glittering bayonets hanging off the saddles of the approaching cavalry troops. She mounted her horse and rode out to meet the soldiers. As she neared the men, they drew their muskets and pointed them at her. She placed her hand over her heart and shouted, "Shoot me, shoot me if you dare! I am not to blame." After a few tense moments, the men lowered their weapons and allowed her to pass. She made her way to the commanding officer to describe what had happened to the peace commission.

The bodies of General Canby and the Reverend Thomas were buried outside the cavalry post. Albert Meacham was removed to the camp hospital. His wounds were pronounced dangerous but not mortal. Winema was among the first to kneel beside his bed. Day after day, she and her husband watched over Meacham until finally he was nursed back to health.

The Modoc War lasted several months. The cavalry launched full-scale attacks against the Modoc braves holed up in the rocks around the army camp. The Natives were determined to hold their ground. Winema went from being the Pocahontas of the territory to Florence Nightingale in the hospital. She tended to the victims of her cousin's bullets, bathing their burning brows and feeding them food she had prepared herself. She protected and cared for the Modoc women and children who were taken captive by the army, too. On many occasions, Winema was asked by the cavalry commander to leave her post and go on with her life. She always refused, noting that some of the white men would seek revenge on the women whose only crime was that of being the mothers of the Modoc warriors resisting the army.

On May 22, 1873, the US cavalry finally broke the Modocs, and the braves surrendered, offering to lead the soldiers to Captain Jack. The Indian chief and five other warriors were arrested for the murders of General Canby and the Reverend Eleasar Thomas. They were tried, found guilty, and sentenced to death.

Despite the attack on his life, Albert Meacham went on to be a champion of Native American rights. He later published a full story of the events surrounding the last days of the Modoc War. He created a lecture-play entitled *Winema* and organized a dramatic troupe to act out the life of "the courageous Indian woman who saved him from certain death." The troupe was made up of Winema, her husband, Frank, their son, Charka, and a number of other Modoc members. The story of her courageous acts and patriotism would transform her into a celebrity.

Meacham's troupe kicked off his tour with a performance in Sacramento City, California. Newspaper accounts indicate the reception was quite favorable: "Honorable Albert Meacham was greeted at the Metropolitan Theatre last night by a large and highly intelligent audience. With arms outstretched he introduced his cast which included a Modoc woman named Winema. Mr. Meacham paid a glowing tribute to the devotion, truth, and sagacity of Winema, and declared her a heroine of the highest order, reciting her deeds briefly, the audience applauded warmly."

After only one show in the West, the troupe went on to conquer the East Coast. They toured for seven years, traveling from New York to New Orleans and points in between. President Ulysses S. Grant held a parade in Winema's honor when she came through Washington, DC.

Following the tour, Winema returned to the Modoc Reservation in Oregon to live the rest of her life. In 1890, she was granted a pension by the federal government as a reward for her years of work to bring about peace. She donated most of the money to her people. She died at the age of seventy-two and was buried in Modoc Cemetery. A national forest in south-central Oregon is named for the tenacious woman chief.

CHAPTER 8

Elizabeth Custer

Champion of the Seventh

*With my husband's departure my last days in the garrison were
ended, as a premonition of disaster that I had never known before
weighed me down. I could not shake off the baleful influence of
depressing thought. This presentiment and suspense, such as I had
never known, made me selfish, and I shut into my heart the most
uncontrollable anxiety, and could lighten no one else's burden.*
—ELIZABETH BACON CUSTER, JUNE 24, 1876

IT WAS ALMOST TWO IN THE MORNING, AND ELIZABETH CUSTER,
the young wife of the famed "boy general"* George, couldn't sleep.
The heat kept her awake—a sweltering intense heat that had over-
taken Fort Lincoln in the Dakota Territory earlier that day. Even if
the conditions had been more congenial, however, sleep would have
eluded Elizabeth. The rumor that had swept through the army post
around lunchtime disturbed her greatly, and, until this rumor was
confirmed, she doubted that she'd be able to get a moment's rest.

---

* Throughout George Custer's military career, his rank bounced from brigadier general, to major
general, to captain, and finally to lieutenant colonel. No matter what his rank really was, he was consistently referred to as general by many civilians and soldiers.

Elizabeth Custer sitting beside her husband, George Armstrong Custer. Her brother-in-law Thomas Custer stands behind the couple. LIBRARY OF CONGRESS

Elizabeth, or Libbie as her husband and friends called her, carried her petite, slender frame over to the window and gazed out at the night sky. It had been more than two weeks since she had said good-bye to her husband. She left him and his battalion a few miles outside the fort. George had orders from his superior officers in Washington, DC, to "round up the hostile Indians in the territory and bring about stability in the hills of Montana." Elizabeth knew he would do everything in his power to fulfill his duty.

George and Elizabeth said their good-byes, and she headed back to the fort. As she rode away, she turned around for one last glance at General Custer's column departing in the opposite direction. It was a splendid picture. The flags and pennons were flying, the men were waving, and even the horses seemed to be arching themselves to show how fine and fit they were. George rode to the top of the promontory and turned around, stood up in his stirrups, and waved his hat. They all started forward again and in a few seconds disappeared—horses, flags, men, and ammunition all on their way to the Little Bighorn River. That was the last time Elizabeth saw her husband alive.

Over and over again, she played out the events of the hot day that had made her restless. She and several other wives had been sitting on the porch of her quarters singing, reluctant for some inexplicable reason to go inside. All at once they noticed a group of soldiers congregating and talking excitedly. One of the Native scouts, a man named Horn Toad, ran to them and announced, "Custer killed. Whole command killed." The women stared at Horn Toad in stunned silence. Finally, one of the wives asked the man how he knew that Custer was killed. He replied, "Speckled Cock, Indian scout, just come. Rode pony many miles. Pony tired. Indian tired. Say Custer shot himself at end. Say all dead."

Elizabeth remembered George's warning about trusting in rumors. She believed that there might have been a skirmish but felt it unlikely that an entire command could be wiped out. At that moment, she refused to believe George would ever dare die. She would wait for confirmation before she did anything else. Now, in her bedroom, listening to the chirping of the crickets and the howls of the coyotes, she sat up, wide awake, waiting.

The loud sound of boots tromping across the path toward her front door gave her a start. She hurried to the door and threw it open. Captain William S. McCaskey entered her home, holding his hat in his hands. He didn't want to be there. Elizabeth looked at him with eyes pleading. "None wounded, none missing, all dead," he sadly reported. Elizabeth stood frozen for a moment, unable to move, the color drained from her face.

"I'm sorry, Mrs. Custer," the captain sighed. "Do you need to sit down?"

Elizabeth blinked away the tears. "No," she replied. "What about the other wives?"

"We'll let them know of their husbands' fates," he assured her.

Despite the intense heat, Elizabeth was now shivering. She picked up a nearby wrap and draped it around her shoulders. Her hands were shaking. "I'm coming with you," she said, choking back the tears. "As the wife of the post commander it's my duty to go along with you when you tell the other . . . widows." The captain didn't argue with the bereaved woman. He knew there would be no point. Elizabeth Custer was as stubborn as her general husband—if not more so.

Despite the heartbreak and privation Elizabeth Custer experienced traveling with her husband from army post to army post, she never regretted the life she had chosen for herself. She preferred living in a tent and making her way across the plains in a covered wagon to "the humdrum life of domestic cares." Elizabeth was the first officer's wife to follow her husband's regiment, and in so doing she changed the image of army wives forever.

Prior to Elizabeth Custer's arrival on the scene, military wives were seldom, if ever, heard from and, in many circles, considered a distraction. Soldiers were encouraged to leave their spouses behind and never discuss their careers with their wives. Elizabeth felt the notion was archaic. She believed a forceful, yet kindly presence in a husband's work could only enhance his career. Much of the career support George received from military leaders was due in part to Elizabeth. She charmed many senators, congressmen, and officers into backing the "boy general" and his lofty ambition of conquering the West.

From the first days of their marriage during the Civil War, the Custers lived together in military encampments whenever possible. Separation, though often unavoidable, was agony. "It is infinitely worse to be left behind, a prey to all the horrors of imagining what may be happening to the ones we love," she recalled in one of her books. "My place is by my husband's side, wherever he may be."

Elizabeth Clift Bacon was born on April 8, 1842. She was one of four children born to Judge Daniel Bacon and his wife, Eleanor Sophia Page. Before Elizabeth had turned eight, her siblings had died of cholera and other related diseases, leaving her an only child.

Days after Elizabeth turned twelve, her mother died of dysentery. It was an event that would weigh heavily on her heart and mind for the rest of her life. Since the age of ten, she had kept a journal. An entry dated August 27, 1854, recalled the tragic day of her mother's funeral. ". . . [M]y mother was laid in the cold ground and as I stood by that open grave and felt—oh! God only knows what anguish filled my heart. O! Why did they put my mother in that great black coffin and screw the lid down so tight [*sic*]? I hope the Lord will spare me to my father for I am his only comfort left."

Daniel was quite protective of his daughter. He kept a close eye on all her activities. The older she got, the more beautiful she became. Eligible young men constantly sought her affections, but the judge was very particular about whom Elizabeth was able to see. He looked out not only for her physical safety but for her emotional well-being, too. When George Custer, an ambitious, young soldier for the Union army, expressed an interest in Elizabeth, Daniel had strong objections. He thought Custer was too outspoken and brash for his genteel daughter. Oddly enough, these were the very qualities Elizabeth found appealing.

The unlikely pair met at a party in late November 1862. Elizabeth knew George by reputation, since he had achieved some distinction as an aide to General George McClellan. Custer was so smitten with Elizabeth that he walked up and down her street, hoping she would step out onto her porch so he could catch a glimpse of her. After a lengthy engagement, the two were married in front of more than three hundred guests at the First Presbyterian Church in Monroe County, Michigan.

By the time Elizabeth and George exchanged vows, the immodest young soldier had been promoted to brigadier general. The newlyweds traveled to various military posts from Cleveland to Washington, DC, attending elaborate balls and parades before settling down to married life. George was ordered to join his command at Stevensburg, Virginia. The Custers' quarters consisted of three upstairs rooms in a farmhouse that was also headquarters for the post. Elizabeth made their home comfortable using furnishings left behind by other post commanders' wives and camping equipment supplied by the army.

Elizabeth accompanied George in the field as often as she could and whenever it was reasonably safe to do so. Small and slender with delicate features, Mrs. Custer seemed physically unfit for life among the tents. Spiritually, she was up to the challenge. She found nontraditional camp life invigorating. From 1866 to 1873, the Custers were stationed at military posts throughout the plains. George was eventually named lieutenant colonel of the Seventh Cavalry Regiment and, in 1873, was ordered to the Dakota Territory to protect railway surveyors and gold miners who were crossing land owned by the Sioux. As she had done in the past, Elizabeth accompanied her husband to this unsettled region.

A late blizzard trapped the cavalry en route to its destination at Yankton in the Dakota Territory. Upon reaching the remote outpost, George and several other soldiers became deathly ill with colds and flu. Custer ordered wives traveling with the regiment out of the camp to protect them from getting sick, but Elizabeth refused to go. She stayed with her husband, determined to nurse him back to health. She cared for twelve other ailing soldiers as well. Because she had no liquor to warm the troops, she gave them alcohol normally used in little spirit lamps, a form of camp stove, and wrapped the men in carpets intended for her quarters. Elizabeth remained strong throughout the ordeal, breaking down only after the snow ended and rescuers arrived to assist the troops. No lives were lost, but many of the men had to have their fingers and toes amputated because of frostbite. Her memoirs indicate that things could have been much worse for them all had they not been with the Seventh Cavalry: "I was thankful that ours was a mounted regiment on one account: if we had belonged to the infantry, the regiment would have had to endure this kind of event more frequently. The horses were too valuable to have their lives endangered by encountering a blizzard, while it was believed that an enlisted man had enough pluck and endurance to bring him out of a storm in one way or another."

Elizabeth's presence alongside her husband in the field was considered new territory for women. She broke conventionalism, considering it better to "face the dangers of the wilds than the sorrow of being left behind." Records from the Kansas State Historical Society show that she redefined the role of the military wife, helping establish wives as valuable assets to their spouses' military careers. Before Elizabeth, women simply accepted the fact that they were in a bigamous relationship. They had married not only a man but also a military system that officially considered them nothing more than camp followers, second always to the mission and the "needs of the service." Elizabeth fought hard to change that perception, stating that "we Army women feel . . . we are important to our husband's work and that we are making history with our men."

Not only was Elizabeth a pioneer of the idea that frontier wives should be involved in their husbands' careers, but she acted on that notion often. One such instance occurred in June 1876. George and Elizabeth were riding at the head of a column en route to Fort Rice in the Dakota Territory, hundreds of miles north of Fort Lincoln, when they unintentionally galloped into a Sioux village.

George calmly greeted the Indians in the camp with "How." The warriors eyed the pair warily. Elizabeth looked on, her eyes fixed on the trail ahead. The two were allowed to pass through the camp without incident. Once the couple was out of sight of the Natives, Elizabeth dismounted her ride and fainted. George brought her around and suggested she return to the column for safety. She dismissed the thought outright and continued with her husband, believing her place was by his side whatever the circumstances. The harrowing experience on the march served only to heighten her self-confidence. She later wrote, "When a woman has come out of danger she is too utterly a coward by nature not to dread enduring the same thing again; but it is something to know she is equal to it. Even though she may tremble and grow faint in anticipation, having once been through it, she can count on rising to the situation when the hour actually comes."

Setting up house and making their quarters comfortable was considered by George to be a heroic feat. Given the raw materials with which Elizabeth and the other army wives had to work, the job was indeed a difficult one. She attempted to beautify their rough furnishings by covering packing boxes with heavy, unglazed cotton fabric, tacking calico over shelves, fastening family photos to the walls to relieve the bareness, and decorating the windows with pressed ferns.

Elizabeth believed that good, home-cooked food helped bolster George's morale, but she struggled to prepare a variety of meals. Eggs were scarce—entire summers would pass where no eggs could be had at all. "The cookbooks were exasperating," she complained. Recipes often called for eggs, butter, and cream, ingredients hard to come by most of the time. "Oh, how I prayed," Elizabeth later recalled, "that some clever army women would prepare a little cooking manual for housekeepers stranded on the frontier."

Elizabeth took her domestic duties seriously, but, because she was an officer's wife, she regarded her social responsibility of equal importance. She did her best to create a harmonious environment at the forts for officers and post visitors. The Custers often hosted dinners and card parties. Twice a month they gave "hops" at which waltzes were featured. At other times, she organized outings to theatrical productions put on by the enlisted men. Elizabeth had political aspirations for George and felt planning these kinds of engagements was great practice for the life they hoped to lead after his military tour.

Elizabeth earned the respect and admiration of many of the officers in George's command. Thomas Custer, her brother-in-law and the Seventh Cavalry's first lieutenant, believed her to be "a most capable soldier's wife." In addition to her camp duties as the colonel's wife, she was called upon to watch over the military payroll of more than $70,000 and assisted in a few bison hunts whenever the regiment was shorthanded.

Some historians consider that her greatest contribution to army life was realized through her writing. She authored three books on the subject of life on the new frontier, describing momentous military events and providing readers with a detailed look at the Wild West.

Elizabeth Custer's account of the death of two civilian men in Yellowstone captured the imminent danger lying in wait for pioneers and soldiers alike who ventured into hostile Native American territory. The slain men had been employed at the post. One was a blacksmith and the other a veterinarian; both had families and devoted wives. They ignored warnings about riding alone outside the fort and met their demise when they stopped to water their horses. A year and a half later, a Native who was gathering supplies at the camp was heard bragging about the murders. His Hunkpapa name was Rain-in-the-Face. He left Fort Lincoln without incident and headed north toward Fort Rice. General Custer secretly sent out a courier to the commander of the fort with direction to assist him in the capture of the desperado. It was Custer's brother, Tom, who identified Rain-in-the-Face among the more than five hundred Hunkpapa on hand at Fort Rice drawing their monthly rations. Elizabeth described the events in her book *Boots and Saddles*:

Colonel Tom came suddenly up behind the Indian. Rain-in-the-Face threw up his arms and Tom seized his Winchester rifle.

He was taken entirely by surprise. Although he showed no fear, his characteristically stolid face flashed hate and revenge for an instant. He drew himself up in an independent manner to show his brother warriors that he did not dread death.

The soldiers tied his hands and stood guard over him. About thirty Indians surrounded them instantly, and one old orator commenced an harangue to the others, inciting them to recapture their brother. Breathless excitement prevailed. At that moment the captain in command appeared in their midst. With the same coolness he had shown in the war and during the six years of his Indian campaigns, he spoke to them through an interpreter. With prudence and tact he explained that they intended to give the prisoner exactly the treatment a white man would receive under like circumstances. Nothing would induce them to give him up and the better plan, to save bloodshed, would be for the chiefs to withdraw and take with them their followers. Seeing that they could accomplish nothing by intimidation or by superior numbers, they had recourse to parley and proposed to compromise. They offered as a sacrifice two Indians of the tribe in exchange for Rain-in-the-Face.

The prisoner was taken back to Fort Lincoln. General Custer's men were prepared for an attack, but none came. Elizabeth was on hand to witness George's interrogation of the Indian and hear the man's confession.

General Custer sent for Rain-in-the-Face. He was tall, straight, and young. His face was quite imperturbable. Through an interpreter, and with every clever question and infinite patience the General spent hours trying to induce the Indian to acknowledge his crime. The culprit's face finally lost its impervious look and he showed some agitation. He gave a brief account of the murder, and the next day made a full confession before all the officers. He said neither of the white men was armed when attacked. He had shot the blacksmith, but he did not die instantly, riding a short distance before falling from his horse. He then went to him and with his stone mallet beat out the last breath left. Before leaving him he shot his body full of arrows. The other man signaled to them from among the bushes, and they knew that the manner in which he held up his hand was an overture of peace. When he reached him the white man gave him his hat as another and further petition for mercy, but he shot him at once, first with his gun and then with arrows. One of the latter entering his back, the dying man struggled to pull it through. Neither man was scalped.

Rain-in-the-Face was placed in a guardhouse with a citizen who had been caught stealing grain from the fort storehouse. The two were chained together. When the thief eventually broke the chain that bound them and escaped, Rain-in-the-Face did the same. He chose not to return to the reservation but joined Sitting Bull, waiting for his chance at revenge on the Seventh Cavalry and, specifically, Tom Custer.

Rain-in-the-Face blamed Colonel Custer for his arrest and seized the opportunity to pay Tom back on June 25, 1876, at the Battle of Little Bighorn. Elizabeth was devastated by the Indian's actions: "The vengeance of that incarnate fiend was concentrated on the man who had effected his capture. It was found on the battlefield that he had cut out the brave heart of the gallant, loyal, and lovable man, my brother Tom."

Night fell over the distraught Fort Lincoln residence. Several days had passed since the camp had been notified of the death of General Custer and all his field soldiers. Elizabeth sat in the dining room of her quarters poring over letters and telegrams of condolences, her face wet with tears. She hadn't slept through the night since the news of her beloved husband's death had been confirmed. Colonel Nelson Miles, commander at Fort Hays, Kansas, paid a visit to the grieving woman. According to historical records, Elizabeth barely spoke to him. When he left the young widow, he pronounced to his wife, Mary, that "Elizabeth's despondency posed an alarming threat to her physical and mental health."

Elizabeth turned to her cousin Rebecca for comfort. The two had written letters to each other for years, and Elizabeth counted on her for sound advice and guidance. Rebecca's kind correspondence about George's death helped her cousin through the most difficult period of her life and gave her the strength to go on. In one letter Rebecca wrote:

> [B]ear bravely the trial of a few years separation from our friends for the sake of the far more exceeding weight of glory which they are thereby crowned. How much rather would you be the early widow of such a man like George Armstrong Custer, than the lifelong wife of many another.
>
> You were a good, true, faithful wife to Armstrong. You gave him domestic happiness and helped make his professional life a success. So, Libbie, your heart's desire in one respect, it seems, was accomplished. His literary reputation was made; his military record was unrivaled . . . his exit from the stage has been even more unexpected and brilliant than the entrance; it was all in character; I believe he had finished his appointed role.

Elizabeth managed to pull herself together and begin a new life without George. She visited the post hospital and helped care for the wounded men. She prayed with them, read to them, and tended to their needs. When Rebecca read about her work in the papers, she immediately wrote her cousin, praising her for her efforts: "I think the mantle of your heroic husband has fallen upon your shoulders. Wear it, Libbie, for his sake!"

Elizabeth set her sights on living out her days as a hero's widow. Everywhere she went she was inundated with praise for George's legacy and asked discreet questions about his life and work. She was the soul of diplomacy and tact until the day George was accused of a soldier's gravest sin—disobedience. Custer's commanding officers set off the controversy, leaking to the public a report stating that the general had waged the attack on the Sioux before so ordered. Elizabeth was furious. The notion that George would lead 261 men to be slaughtered solely on his own orders was offensive to his memory. She would be the one to speak out in defense of her husband's work.

Elizabeth was not only burdened with defending George's military career but also forced to deal with speculations centering on his gambling habit. Custer did indeed have a problem. Only after his death did Elizabeth learn that he owed thousands of dollars in gambling debts. It was one of George's flaws that she refused to discuss with anyone. After selling his estate to make good on those debts, she was left virtually penniless.

Strapped for money and driven by the need to defend her husband's reputation, Elizabeth decided to write a book about her life with Custer. She relocated to New York and began work on the manuscript. She supplemented the income she received from the army widows' fund with paid lectures describing the domestic life of the cavalry at frontier outposts. In March 1885, Elizabeth's first book was in bookstores. Entitled *Boots and Saddles: Life in Dakota with General Custer*, the small volume was dedicated to "My Husband: The Echo of Whose Voice Has Been My Inspiration." *Boots and Saddles* extolled Custer's virtues as a soldier and patriot and promptly silenced his critics. Her next book, *Tenting in the Plains*, was another glowing testament to George Custer's character and superior work as a dedicated leader of the Seventh Cavalry.

Those who dared speak out against the widow Custer's second volume accused her of embellishing George's contributions. Major Marcus Reno, one of Custer's staunchest critics, accused the general of being arrogant and reckless. According to Reno's memoirs, the defeat of the Seventh Cavalry was due entirely to Custer. "He failed to follow orders," Reno wrote, "dividing the regiment without adequate reconnaissance and finally, the soldier's fatigue from forced marching."

He wasn't alone in his opinion of Custer. Although several years had passed since the Battle of Little Bighorn, the reason for Custer's last stand was still the subject of debate and controversy. Elizabeth remained firm in her campaign to preserve George's legacy. When Reno died of throat cancer, there was no one left to challenge her publicly.

With Elizabeth's third book, *Following the Guidon*, she firmly established George as a brilliant military commander and a family man without personal failings. At this point, scholars in the New York Public Library archives department argued that she was defending the myth she had created—a myth upon which she was financially and emotionally dependent.

Fifty years after the death of her husband, Elizabeth Custer was lobbying Congress for a museum at the Little Bighorn Battlefield. She believed the men who lost their lives in that conflict should be recognized for their heroism. Over the years, she monitored the maintenance of the Custer Battlefield National Cemetery but was driven to create a more lasting memorial for the fallen soldiers. She never saw her dream realized.

Elizabeth Bacon Custer died four days before her ninety-first birthday in 1933. In one of her last recollections to a good friend, she noted, "The hours that one sees people and keeps up the farce of perpetual happiness are few compared with the never ending hours when one is alone with the past, and all those who were nearest have 'gone to the country from which no traveller [*sic*] returns.'"

CHAPTER 9

Lozen

The Warrior Shaman

Lozen is my right hand . . . strong as a man, braver than most, and cunning in strategy. Lozen is a shield to her people.
—APACHE WAR CHIEF VICTORIO, JUNE 1880

THE APACHE LEADER KNOWN AS GERONIMO STOOD NEAR AN overhanging cliff in the Chiricahua Mountains of Arizona studying the terrain before him. His keen eye traveled across the rocks and valley below. It was unlikely the US cavalry would track the fugitive into the rocky stronghold, but Geronimo didn't like to underestimate the army's tenacity. A band of thirty-six loyal warriors surrounded the courageous renegade, ready to defend their lives and land should the military be in the immediate area and dare attack the party. Geronimo fixed his gaze on a distant plateau and lifted his voice to the sky. "We have suffered much from the unjust orders of US generals," he said. "Such acts have caused much distress to my people. We will defend what is ours to the last man."

A cold stillness hung in the air—a sense of impending calamity marking the beginning of the end of a race of people. Suddenly all eyes turned to an unassuming medicine woman stepping out of a cave in a massive pile of lava rocks. She walked over to an outcropping of stone and bowed her head.

Geronimo watched with great interest as Lozen stretched her arms out and turned her palms to the heavens. She was petite and plain, her skin as supple as leather and her manner of dress in keeping with the other warriors. She scanned the horizon as the braves waited. They dared not make a move without Lozen's wise council. It was her divine power that had kept Geronimo and his followers out of harm's way for so long. Without her ability to detect the enemy's nearing presence, the Apaches would have perished.

For close to a year, Geronimo's desperate band of braves eluded US Army scouts. These few Natives were the last of the free Apaches—stubborn holdouts who refused to surrender, be forced from their land, and be placed on a reservation. Many believed it was better to die like warriors than live off the scraps like dogs from the emigrants they referred to as "white eyes." Lozen honored the beliefs of her people and used her gift to keep the "white eyes" at bay.

Geronimo watched Lozen tightly close her eyes. A gust of wind swept over her small frame, tossing about her straight, dark hair. "Can you tell me if the soldiers are near?" he asked quietly.

"I can," she replied. She stood in silence for a moment, her arms further extended, her hands slightly cupped. "The god Ussen has given me this power . . . it is good, as he is good," she exclaimed.

Geronimo and his men looked on, anxiously awaiting Lozen's answer. When she opened her eyes, they glittered. The power with which she had been blessed often moved her to tears; she felt unworthy of such a great gift. She turned to the proud faces of the expectant warriors, and her eyes peered into Geronimo's. "Rest easy," she told him. "No enemy is near this night."

Lozen was born a member of the Mimbres tribe of Apache in 1840. Her family lived near Ojo Caliente in New Mexico. Her father was a leading member of his band, and her mother was a well-respected woman. Not unlike most Indian children at that time, Lozen learned to ride a horse when she was very young. By the age of eight, she was considered

Lozen, top row, center
NATIONAL ANTHROPOLOGICAL ARCHIVES, SMITHSONIAN INSTITUTION

an expert rider. From early on it was clear to her parents that she would not assume the traditional female role. She loved hunting and playing rough games with her brother, Victorio, and the other boys in the tribe. Her skills with a bow and arrow and a sling were exceptional. Like her father and his father before him, she was a born warrior.

Lozen's homeland, a stretch of ground that encompassed parts of New Mexico, Arizona, and northern Mexico, was rich with gold. The Mexicans were the first to invade the territory and try to possess the precious metal. They came by the hundreds, feverishly digging into the earth like coyotes. When they tired of searching for the nuggets themselves, they made slaves of some Cheyenne and Apache people in the area. Indian leaders quickly formed raiding parties in an effort to take back the land the Mexicans occupied and to free the Native slaves. Among them was Mangas Coloradas, chief of the Mimbreno Chiricahuas, as well as Cochise, Geronimo, and, in time, Lozen's brother, Victorio. Each pledged to resist the colonization of their native soil by the Spaniards and the incursion of white fortune seekers on their way to California.

Lozen's young eyes witnessed numerous battles and countless brutal deaths. Often Apaches were slaughtered during so-called peace negotiations between Indian council members and the gold seekers. They sought revenge for every life that was taken at the hands of their enemies. Mexican prisoners were occasionally taken and would be led out bound and gagged before the tribe. Then the wives, daughters, and mothers of the murdered Apache would kill the men. Lozen watched them cut the miners into pieces with knives or crush their skulls under the weight of their horses. Eventually the harsh retaliation forced the Mexicans to abandon the area and retreat south. Troubles for the Apaches, however, were far from over. They were warned by other tribes that the white eyes were coming and were like the leaves on the trees—too numerous to number.

Before the white eyes overtook their land and many Native traditions were abandoned, Lozen would learn about the remarkable Apache women who had gone before her. They were shamans and warriors, mothers and hunters—women she admired and longed to emulate. Shortly after her coming-of-age ceremony was celebrated by the tribe, Lozen journeyed to the sacred mountain to ask god for a gift to help her people. It was a ritual all Indian women went through. While at the sacred mountain, she was given the power to understand horses and the ability to hear and see the enemy. If an enemy was near, she would feel his presence in the heat of her palms when she faced the direction from which he would come. She could determine the distance of the enemy by the intensity of the heat. The Apaches sorely needed a woman with Lozen's unique talent; they didn't have enough warriors or enough power to battle the overwhelming white invaders.

Among the important influences in Lozen's life was her older brother, Victorio. From boyhood he had been groomed to be chief of the Chiricahua Apache tribe. He was blessed with the power of war and the handling of men. Tall and imposing, he was respected by all members of the band and referred to by other leaders as the perfect warrior. Lozen rode with Victorio and served as his apprentice. The two combined their powers and led warriors on many successful raids against white prospectors who attacked peaceful Apache camps. Nothing they did could stem the tide of settlers entering their country.

The ground covering the western territories was soaked with the blood of Natives and ambitious pioneers alike. The US government sent soldiers to the Southwest and built army posts where needed to give settlers protection along the Santa Fe Trail. Presidents Ulysses S. Grant and Rutherford B. Hayes sent envoys to the various Indian nations to negotiate peace and prevent further war. Lozen and Victorio attended those meetings, but they were wary of the promises made by the white leaders. In time the US government broke all agreements made with the Apaches and forced Lozen and the other Chiricahuas onto the Warm Springs Apache Reservation in San Carlos, Arizona.

San Carlos was a hellishly hot, desert land, and the Chiricahuas were unable to grow crops there as they had when they resided in the Mimbres Mountains. They could not provide for themselves and had to depend on the government for food and supplies. Between the hungry tribe and provisions, however, stood the corrupt government agents working at the reservation who were stealing funds meant for the Indians to purchase food.

Victorio appealed to General John Howard, an Indian agent overseeing the Apaches' transition from plains living to the reservation, and requested that his people be returned to their homeland. Howard agreed to take the matter to President Grant. Lozen waited by her brother's side for word from the government. Two years passed before the appeal was officially granted.

The Apaches' time in Ojo Caliente was short-lived. Government rations set aside for the tribe were diverted again, and, when the Natives began stealing from the settlers, the army quickly rounded them up and marched them back to San Carlos. Conditions at the Warm Springs Reservation had not improved since they'd last been there. Not only was the lack of supplies still a problem, but outbreaks of malaria and smallpox were now claiming the lives of hundreds of Chiricahuas. Victorio called together the Apache leaders for a council meeting. Lozen was the only woman allowed.

After much discussion, Victorio and Geronimo decided to leave the reservation, taking with them all who wanted to return to New Mexico. On September 2, 1877, a band of 320 Apaches fled Warm Springs. Lozen was among them.

Lozen and Victorio raided camps as they traveled. They killed herders, mules, and steers, stopping only long enough to cut the animal meat. Lozen's powers protected the band from the enemy's fast approach. Soldiers eventually overtook the group and tried to persuade them to return to the reservation. The brother-and-sister team was warned that any Indian found off the reservation would be killed.

"We'll not be killed; we'll be free," Lozen replied. "What is life if we are imprisoned like cattle in a corral?"

Lozen's words inspired her brother. He vowed to stay and fight to return to his homeland. A warrant was quickly issued for his arrest. The Apaches waged war against troops who tried to bring their chief to justice. The desperate band kept themselves alive and thwarted army capture by stealing food and horses. They ran from and fought off both American and Mexican soldiers and survived on the run for three years at various spots in Texas, Arizona, New Mexico, and Mexico.

Throughout the Chiricahuas' trials and conflicts, Lozen proved herself a valuable warrior and scout. At times she even acted as an interpreter between Victorio and the frustrated cavalry. She tended to Victorio's occasional injuries and helped his wives with their children. In mid-October 1880, a Mescalero Indian woman traveling with Victorio's band went into labor. Victorio and his followers risked being caught by the soldiers if they stopped. The chief instructed Lozen to stay back with the woman and see her through the birth. She reluctantly agreed.

Lozen led the mother-to-be along an overgrown trail to an isolated spot away from the river. In the near distance she caught a glimpse of a contingency of army troops headed their way. Lozen sought to hide their position in a clump of thick brush as the Mescalero's baby would arrive at the same time as the scouts and soldiers.

Lozen helped the woman into the foliage and, when she was sure they could not be seen, allowed the expectant mother to deliver. Lozen laid a rifle across her lap and watched with careful eyes as the cavalry approached. She placed a hand over the Mescalero woman's mouth to muffle her sounds of pain. Once the baby came, Lozen cut the cord with a piece of black flint, then tied off the stub of the cord with a piece of yucca string.

The baby boy whimpered only a little. Lozen whispered a prayer over him and gave him to his mother. She held her gun at the ready and peered out the brush at the soldiers. One of the scouts seemed to be looking in their direction. She placed a finger on the trigger of the gun. If he got too near, she would have to shoot. Just before the scout reached the three, he stopped, turned around, and rode off. Lozen, the mother, and her son were left alone.

Lozen continued to feel the presence of the enemy long after they had disappeared from sight. Her thoughts centered on her brother and the warriors with him. An uneasiness filled her heart and mind. In that moment she wished she had defied her brother and stayed with him. She sensed he needed her now more than ever.

Victorio and his band of loyal followers, meantime, were riding hard into Mexican territory, hoping to lead US troops away from the mountains and onto the plains. On their way to a place called Tres Castillos, the Indians were ambushed by Mexican soldiers. Victorio and more than a hundred other Apaches were killed. Sixty-eight were captured and sold as slaves. Only seventeen Chiricahuas managed to escape.

When Lozen reached the Mescalero Reservation, she learned of her brother's death at the Battle of Tres Castillos. She was heartsick, convinced that had she been with him the group never would have been surprised. Apache leader Nana comforted Lozen by reminding her that Victorio "died as he lived, free and unconquerable." Nana's words helped, but Lozen would never be the same. Inspired by her brother's drive to spare his people the ignominy of imprisonment and slavery, Lozen, along with the remaining Natives, prepared to do the only thing they knew: to fight and die as warriors. After several months battling with Mexican and US soldiers, Nana led the tired handful of warriors, their wives, and their children back to the San Carlos Reservation. At San Carlos the band could rest, accumulate food and supplies, and recruit more warriors.

Lozen and the dedicated tribesmen who wanted to live again on their own land joined forces with Geronimo, then left the reservation, and headed south toward the Sierra Madre. As the party traveled, Geronimo consulted Lozen's powers just as Victorio had done. The band raided sheep and cattle ranches to sustain themselves while on the run. Geronimo devised a plan of attack on forty men serving as cavalry police and scouts. With those men out of the way, Geronimo determined he could move about Apache land undetected. A plan was also set to destroy telegraph wires so communication between army posts would be minimized. One by one the scouts and police fell at the hands of Geronimo's warriors.

Geronimo relied greatly on Lozen to keep his braves from danger. Without her help the Apache would not have met their objective. For a while the Natives were happy camped in the Chiricahua Mountains, but more settlers were pouring into the wilderness, and for their safety the government would not allow the determined Apaches to continue their actions. Over time, the Mexican and US troops managed to track and capture a number of renegade Apaches until only thirty-six were left on the run. Lozen and Geronimo were among them.

In August 1886, the Chiricahua tribe was backed against the wall. With so few members left to take up the cause for freedom and the lack of food and supplies taking its toll on the last of the holdouts, Geronimo was faced with the decision to surrender to the white eyes. General Nelson A. Miles was sent to negotiate Geronimo's surrender. He was hesitant at first, but Lozen convinced him to sit down and talk with the soldiers. "Only hardship and death wait for us on the warpath," she told him. Lozen had lived nine years on the run. The white eyes and the Mexicans had chased them without pause. She knew the troops would continue to hunt them until they killed them all, even if it took fifty years.

"Everything is against us now," Lozen said to Geronimo on the eve of his surrender. "If we awake at night and a rock rolls down the mountain or a stick breaks, we will be running. We even eat our meals on the run. On the run you have no friends whatever in the world. But on the reservation we could get plenty to eat, go wherever we want, talk to good people."

Geronimo listened to the military leaders and agreed to stop fighting if they could all return to the reservation and live at Turkey Creek, New Mexico, on farms. General Miles explained that he could only deliver the message to his superior officers and added that this was their last chance to surrender. Geronimo reluctantly agreed to lay down arms.

In retaliation for the Chiricahua Apache's success at resisting imprisonment, the entire tribe—more than five hundred people, most of whom were living on the San Carlos Reservation—was deported from Arizona. Lozen was among the leaders shipped by train from Fort Bowie, Arizona, to Fort Pickens, Florida. US soldiers placed all the Indians in two cars, packing them in like cattle. Many died en route to the coast. Even more succumbed once they reached Florida. Pneumonia, meningitis, and malaria claimed the lives of hundreds of men, women, and children. Army-post doctors also reported deaths due to depression at the conditions.

Lozen never saw her homeland again. She fell victim to tuberculosis and died in late 1890. She was buried in an unmarked grave. Tales of the most famous Chiricahua war woman to ever live continue to be told to young Apache children today.

CHAPTER 10

Sarah Winnemucca

Paiute Princess

In the history of the Indians, she and Pocahontas will be the principal female characters, and her singular devotion to her race will no doubt be chronicled as an illustration of the better traits of the Indian character.

—SAN FRANCISCO CALL, JANUARY 1885

The Bannock War and the Army

Territorial Enterprise, *June 5, 1878: We copy the subjoined article from the Winnemucca* Silver State:

There is no longer any doubt of the uprising of the Bannock Indians. Another war has been inaugurated in Idaho which may prove much more serious than that of the last year, as the Bannocks are far more numerous and range through a larger extent of the territory than the Nez Perces. Troops have been ordered to the scene of hostilities from Walla Walla and Camp Harney, and the cavalry at Halleck have orders to be ready to march at a moment's notice.

Sarah Winnemucca brooded over the abandoned houses along the dusty track. She and her small party had departed the John Day Valley in the eastern Oregon Territory three days before. They were on the way to Silver City, Idaho, where Sarah would drop off her passengers before heading for Elko, Nevada. There she intended to take a train to Washington, DC, and attempt to tell President Rutherford B. Hayes that her people were starving, the Indian agents were crooked, and none of the promises to the Paiute had been kept. On June 8, three days after the war was reported in the *Enterprise*, Sarah was unknowingly headed straight for the heart of the battle. "We saw houses standing all along the road without anybody living in them," Sarah later wrote in her book *Life Among the Piutes* [*sic*].

On June 12, they met Paiute Joe on the road and learned the dreadful news. "He said the Bannock Indians were just killing everything that came in their way, and he told us to get to a place called Stone House. That was the first I heard that the Bannocks were on the warpath." She also learned that there was no one the Bannocks would love to kill more than Chief Winnemucca's daughter.

When the Bannock War broke out, Sarah was thirty-four years old, daughter of the highly respected Paiute chief Winnemucca and granddaughter of old Chief Truckee, who first met Captain John Fremont and his explorers and guided them over the Sierra Mountains. Truckee had for years considered white people the long-lost brothers of Indians and always counseled peace despite increasing violence by whites against his people and the outright theft of Paiute lands in the Nevada Territory.

Now it appeared the Paiutes were caught in a vise between their northern neighbors in Idaho and Oregon, the Bannock Indians, and the increasing number of settlers pushing them out of their tribal lands in Nevada. Also known as the Snake Indians, the Bannocks

Sarah Winnemucca Hopkins, ca. 1883–1890

were superb horsemen, tall and lean. They dressed in fringed buck-skin decorated with quills, scalps, and red, yellow, and black paint and wore a single eagle feather or a headdress made of trimmed horsetail or porcupine skin. Their enemies considered them the most savage and bloodthirsty of all the Indians west of the Missis-sippi, but they had been relatively peaceful until driven to rebellion.

Territorial Enterprise, *June 11, 1878: General [O. O.] How-ard says the Government has not kept faith with the Ban-nocks, and [General] Crook believes they have been starved into insurrection.*

On June 12, 1878, Major Edwin Mason, attached to General Howard's command, wrote to his wife from Boise, Idaho, that mili-tary forces would quickly crush the Bannocks. "We are of the opin-ion that it is only a big spree among the Indians and that a month's good work will knock the bottom out of it."

As Mason headed cheerfully down the trail from Boise, eighty miles as the crow flies, Sarah's small group and Paiute Joe galloped into Stone House, just over the border in eastern Oregon. They were accompanied by approximately twenty scouts. Joe reportedly explained the situation: "The Bannocks are all out fighting. They are killing everything and everybody, Indians and whites, and I and two of my people went with these men to South Mountain to fight them, and we came on to Buffalo Horn's camp and had a fight with them." Paiute Joe, though wounded, managed to kill Buffalo Horn, then jumped on his horse and escaped.

Sarah instantly dropped plans to go to Washington, DC. Instead, in the hope of aiding a peace effort, she offered her ser-vices as interpreter to the army. The offer was greeted with great suspicion. Citizens at Stone House believed her wagon was loaded with ammunition intended for the Bannocks. Even the soldiers who arrived with Captain Reuben Bernard "looked at me as if I were some fearful beast." She spent the night locked inside the hotel, while citizens armed with rifles watched the wagon. The next morning, she demanded Bernard search it. "Go and see for yourself, Captain," she cried, "and if you find anything in my wagon besides a knife and fork and a pair of scissors I will give you my head for your football."

Bernard believed her and realized she could be an asset to the army. Although only about five feet tall, she rode a horse as well as any man he had seen, even when seated sidesaddle when she wished to show she was a lady. Her training as a youngster had included a stint in a California school as well as residence in the household of a Nevada family where she learned to read and write. That training had been put to good use at the Malheur Reservation where her people had been removed, but she'd been fired from her job and banished for reporting the Indian agent's theft of blankets and the starvation rations he provided for her people. Those trials and others had motivated her now-aborted attempts to seek justice in Washington.

Worried about her family, Sarah waited to hear the latest news of the war. When a dispatch arrived at Stone House from Camp McDermitt, Sarah volunteered to take the news to Sheep Ranch, some thirty miles away. Garbed in a riding habit and riding side-saddle, Sarah and a small escort galloped across the sage-covered hills. As they neared the encampment, they saw a man on the road ahead. Apparently believing the Natives meant to attack, the man first ran and then turned to shoot. Fortunately, Sarah and her party were able to reach Sheep Ranch safely. There she was asked to get the Paiute with her to carry a message to Camp Harney or the Malheur Agency to discover the whereabouts of the Bannock.

The request was greeted with uneasiness and brought even more bad news from Paiute Joe. "Sarah, we will do anything we can for the officers and you; we will go with dispatches anywhere but to the hostile Bannocks; we cannot go to them, for, Sarah, you don't know what a danger that is." Sarah knew if the Indians accepted the mission, they could easily be killed. Then, a stunning revelation from the scouts: "Sarah, your brother Natchez was killed, or is dead."

Despite her fear that this awful news might be true, Sarah told Captain Bernard she would do her best to accomplish the mission, even if she had to go alone. Bernard wrote a letter of safe passage: "To all good citizens of the country—Sarah Winnemucca, with two of her people, goes with a dispatch to her father. If her horses should give out, help her all you can."

Territorial Enterprise, *June 13, 1878: It is now conceded that the uprising is almost universal among the Bannocks, and that all the military forces of the Division of the Pacific will be required to subdue the savages.*

With two men at her side, Sarah galloped off toward the crossing of the Owyhee River. A mile beyond the crossing, they struck the Bannocks' trail. "We followed it down the river as much as fifteen miles, and then we came to the place where they had camped, and where they had been weeping, and where they had cut their hair. So we knew that it was hereabout that Buffalo Horn had been killed." Trying not to think about the fate of her brother Natchez, Sarah continued on the trail.

"We rode very hard all day long—did not stop to rest all that day. The country was very rocky and no water. We had traveled about fifty miles that day. Now it was getting dark, but we rode on.

It was very difficult for us to travel fast, for our horses almost fell over sometimes."

The two men and Sarah stopped for the night, eating a little hard bread with no water. She lay down to sleep but kept waking up when the horse she'd tethered to her arm kept pulling on the reins. At dawn they were off again across the Barren Valley, heading for a ranch where there would be water and food. From a distance, they saw the smoke.

The house, still smoldering, had been burned to the ground. They made coffee in a scorched tin can, but Sarah refused to kill and eat any of the loose chickens; they belonged to the absent rancher. The men considered themselves under her command, and she determined to continue on the trail of the Natives headed toward Steens Mountain in southeast Oregon. It was sixty miles to the nearest settlement.

Silver City, Idaho, June 14, 1878: There is general joy here at the prospect of General Crook coming to take a hand in putting down the Indian rebellion. He is very popular in Idaho. Ten whites have thus far been killed by the Bannocks.

The same day, galloping across the barren, sage-covered hill-sides, Sarah unexpectedly met Lee, another of her brothers. "The minute he rode up he jumped from his horse and took me in his arms," Sarah wrote. Lee said their father, Chief Winnemucca, and their people were prisoners of the Bannocks, who had taken their few guns and all their horses. "Have you brought us some good news?" Lee asked, and then realized everyone was in great danger as they stood talking. "The Bannocks are out in the mountains, look-ing out. Take off your hat and your dress and unbraid your hair, and put this blanket round you, so if they should come down they would not know who it is." All three disguised themselves as Bannocks, although that put them in danger from the military and the settlers.

Then Sarah asked the location of her father; she still had the message from General Howard to deliver to him. "Oh, dear sister, you will be killed if you go there, for our brother Natchez made his escape three days ago." Delighted to hear that her brother was alive after all, Sarah did not tarry though she rode straight into grave danger. "I must save my father and his people even if I lose my life in trying to do it," she told Lee.

Climbing a steep mountain, sometimes on hands and knees, they reached the top and looked down into the Bannock encampment. It was a thrilling yet terrifying sight. About 327 lodges and 425 warriors were in the valley. "The place looked like it was all alive and filled with hostile Bannocks. I began to feel a little afraid." Nevertheless, Sarah concocted a plan to get inside the camp, warn Chief Winnemucca and the other Paiutes from the Malheur Agency, and get them all away to the promised safety of General Howard's troops.

Racing down the mountain under as much cover as could be found, they infiltrated the Bannock camp and stole into the tents of the Paiute prisoners. Later, they put Sarah's plan into play. While the Bannocks were busy butchering cattle for an evening feast, the women left the lodges as though to gather wood, and then disappeared. The men slipped out one by one, until only Sarah, her father, Lee, and some Winnemucca cousins remained in the lodge. As darkness fell, they, too, slipped away.

Fearful of discovery, they hurried away from the encampment. Now that she had accomplished her purpose, Sarah's strength finally wavered. "It was like a dream. I could not get along at all. I almost fell down at every step, my father dragging me along. Oh, how my heart jumped when I heard a noise nearby."

The noise was her sister-in-law Mattie, hiding in the brush with a horse. Reunited, the small band left the mountain and met the other Paiutes at Juniper Lake, where the women were cooking a mountain sheep cached there the day before when Sarah and the two men had ascended the mountain. Eating on the run, they rode all night and reached Summit Springs. Sarah had barely laid down to rest when an alarm sounded. A man arrived, his horse nearly foundering under him, to give the warning: The Bannock were right behind. "I looked back," said the messenger, "and saw Lee running, and they firing at him. I think he is killed. Oytes [the Bannock chief] is at the head of this. I heard him say to the Bannocks, 'Go quickly, bring Sarah's head and her father's too. I will show Sarah who I am.'"

The next morning, June 15, Sarah and Mattie separated from the family. They galloped toward General Howard, at least seventy-five miles away over rough, dry country. Chief Winnemucca and his band remained behind to try to save Lee and the others. Her father had asked Sarah to tell Howard to send soldiers to protect the Paiutes who had refused to go to war.

By one o'clock, Sarah and Mattie had reached Muddy Creek, where they watered the horses and ate some white currants growing on the banks. At three o'clock, they reached the crossing at the Owyhee River, where people gave them coffee and hard bread while fresh horses were saddled. "We jumped on our horses again, and I tell you we made our time count going fifteen miles to the Sheep Ranch. We whipped our horses every step of the way until we were met by the officers."

They encountered some disbelief, but finally General Howard ordered a force of men to meet Chief Winnemucca and bring him in. "This was the hardest work I ever did for the government in all my life—the whole round trip from 10 o'clock, June 13, up to June

15, arriving back at 5:30 p.m., having been in the saddle night and day; distance about two hundred twenty-three miles."

Sunday morning, June 16, General Howard asked Sarah to join him as interpreter and guide. Sarah agreed but was "mad as could be" because she wanted to turn around and go after the Bannocks who had imprisoned her family. Howard gave general field orders from Sheep Ranch directing all the forces available toward Steens Mountain: "The enemy is reported in large force. The columns will move with usual military precautions to scout the country and avoid ambuscades."

Sarah and Mattie acted as scouts with Captain Bernard's forces as they traveled toward Camp Lyon and from there to Malheur City. Before they reached the town, news came on June 19 that the Bannocks had abandoned Steens Mountain for Harney Valley. Captain Bernard was hard on their ponies' heels.

"Later in the evening General Howard and Lieutenant Wilkinson came to us again and said, 'Well, Sarah, what do you think about going?'" Once again she agreed to carry a dispatch to Bernard despite danger from both frightened settlers and raiding Indians. With a couple of soldiers as escort, they set out on the morning of the twentieth for Camp Harney, 120 miles away. The small party did not stop to eat until dark and then traveled all night long. They arrived at Camp Harney at ten o'clock the following morning. "Oh, how tired I was! Mattie and I went to bed without anything to eat." They awoke to learn Captain Bernard had finally engaged the enemy.

Silver City, Idaho, June 27: In the recent attack of Captain Bernard's command upon the hostile forces, the force of the latter is said to have been 1,000 warriors. The Indians were not aware of the presence of the soldiers, and their stock was unguarded.

Bernard addressed his troops, informing them that they were very close by the enemy and could whip them. He charged them not to retreat, as, if they did, they would be shot and they might as well die by shots fired by the savages as by their own men.

By one o'clock on the morning of June 24, Bernard had chased the Bannocks another ten miles. General Howard arrived later, along with other troops. Sarah and Mattie followed, once again as guides and interpreters. At one point the volunteers saw what they thought was a large force of Natives on the hills. Sarah disagreed and said there was no danger. Finally, troopers scaled the heights and discovered exactly what Sarah had said would be there: rocks piled to look like people waiting to conduct an ambush.

The twenty-ninth of June saw them high in the mountains, where it snowed all day. The cavalry pursued Bannocks down the canyon of the John Day River while Howard and his wagons lumbered behind, slipping and sliding down steep slopes. Continuing the march, Howard's forces reached Pilot Rock on the Camas Prairie. After studying the terrain, Sarah explained that the hostile Indians were in perfect position for a quick escape, but no one listened.

She was right again. Major Edwin Mason told his wife in a letter dated July 8, "We had a lively fight today." Mason went on to praise Bernard's expertise. "I have rarely seen men handled in better style. They moved to the attack without a moment's hesitation, firing as they advanced, leading their horses up the steep and rocky hill without a particle of cover, for the country is treeless." However, the Bannock escaped into the forest at their backs, as Sarah had predicted.

"I knew they would go into the timber and get away, and this I told the General, but he would not believe it." Nor did he believe her when she said the Bannocks would double back through the

Blue Mountains to the Malheur Agency. That was exactly what happened, and Howard was soon bogged down in the most treacherous terrain possible. The canyon route they followed was twelve hundred feet deep, nearly perpendicular, with the North Fork of the John Day River thundering at the bottom. They slid down the trail to the riverbank and crossed the rushing stream, then climbed the opposite side, leading the horses, "the ascent being so steep that several of our pack animals fell over backwards into the stream and were lost," Sarah later wrote. One skirmish resulted in the death of a courier by a different band of Natives led by Chief Homeli:

Baker City, Oregon, July 17: Chief Homely [sic] with his band of Indians fought hostiles on the 15th instant, killing Chief Egan and have his scalp and head.

"Oh, I saw the most fearful thing during the summer's campaign," Sarah reported. "Poor Egan, who was not for war, was most shamefully murdered by Umatilla Indians. He was cut in pieces by them, and his head taken to the officers, and Dr. Fitzgerald boiled it to get the skull to keep." Sarah mentioned the atrocities in her book but always returned to the tale of her march with the army. She and Mattie accompanied General Forsythe on a rambling, 150-mile circuit, picking up small parties of hostiles.

When they neared Camp McDermitt, Sarah felt the strong pull of family. She talked Forsythe into allowing her to leave, and, though she wanted to go alone, by night, Forsythe insisted she take three men. At six o'clock they departed, riding all night long. Just at daybreak, Sarah raced ahead to the camp where she found her brother Natchez and her father, who held her with tears running down his face. "Oh, my poor child! I thought I would never see you, for the papers said you were killed by the Bannocks."

By August the war was just about over. Sarah made long, hot rides for General Howard, who commended her loyalty. Nevertheless, it was Howard who ordered all the Paiutes at Malheur to the Yakama Reservation in Washington, beyond the Columbia River, far from Winnemucca's original lands in northern Nevada. For the first time, Sarah disobeyed orders. Instead of rounding up Indians to bring back to the camp, she warned them away, but it was too little, and far too late. In December 1878, Sarah and her people began the 350-mile trek to Yakama. Screaming women and children unwilling to march were tossed into wagons; men, shackled by chains, walked through the snow.

February 2, 1879, they arrived in Yakama, where they were quartered in a cattle shed. The snow was waist deep. The Yakama people resented the Paiutes, stole their horses, and threatened the children. The Indian agent described the Paiutes as some of the most destitute of any he had seen, some being literally naked, but he did little more than pray for them. As her people died in the harsh conditions, Sarah was filled with grief. Once more she was persuaded to act on their behalf.

Earning money by lecturing on traditions of her people and speaking eloquently of the conditions they now endured, Sarah raised money for another journey to Washington, DC. The trip to tell the president of her people's troubles that had been interrupted by the news of the Bannock uprising was resumed. In the winter of 1879–1880, she traveled with her father to the nation's capital, where she met with President Hayes and secured promises of better treatment for her people.

Promises easily broken.

They were assured that they could return, at their own expense, to Malheur Reservation. Unfortunately, in 1881, permission to depart was denied by Yakama agent James H. Wilbur, the "blue sky" agent who looked toward heaven and prayed while the Paiute's blankets were stolen right off their slumbering forms.

"Knowing the temper of the people through whom they must pass, still smarting from the barbarities of war two years previous, and that the Paiutes, utterly destitute of everything, must subsist themselves on their route by pillage, I refused permission for them to depart," Wilbur reported. Five years later, many of the Paiutes still remained at the Yakama Reservation, unable to get the money or the permission to leave.

Despite betrayal after betrayal, for the rest of her life Sarah worked for her people. She married William Hopkins but was later divorced. She lectured across the nation, started a school for Indian children, and wrote the first book ever penned by a Native woman, *Life Among the Piutes, Their Wrongs and Claims*, [*sic*] published first in 1883.

The original editor of the book, Mary Peabody Mann, noted that Sarah's speeches were extraordinarily moving, but it was her goal to set down in writing the full story. "It is the first outbreak of the American Indian in human literature, and it has a single aim—to tell the truth as it lies in the heart of a true patriot, and one whose knowledge of the two races gives her an opportunity of comparing them justly."

SARAH WINNEMUCCA
The Death of a Noted Indian Woman,
With a Sketch of Her Somewhat Interesting Life.

Bozeman Chronicle, *October 28, 1891: Sarah Winnemucca Hopkins, well known in this country, after eating a hearty meal on Friday, the 16th, suddenly expired in great pain. This was at Henry's Lake, one hundred and twenty miles away from*

Bozeman, and almost as far away from a doctor. As a result, the nature of the disease which carried this notable woman away, is not, and may never be known.

CHAPTER 11

Calamity Jane

Mysterious Marvel

In the house of terror and death, there came to the front a willing volunteer, the mule-skinning, bull whacking and rough, roving woman from the depths—Calamity Jane.

—ANONYMOUS

COLD RAIN LASHED THE HUDDLE OF TENTS STAKED JUST OUTSIDE the rough encampment at Rapid City. Wind howled across the Dakota Territory as though driven by the devil himself, rattling the dripping canvas and blowing crude shakes from the leaky roofs of the buildings. Struggling through the mud, a young woman leaned into the gale and cursed. The stupidity of setting up a camp for sick soldiers on the lowest ground near General Crook's encampment was enough to make a deacon swear, thought Martha Jane Canary.

The wind tore the tent flap from her grasp. Cursing again, she grabbed the wet canvas and yanked it into place. A lantern swaying from a hook on the tent pole cast meager light on the three men huddled in damp bedrolls. Martha Jane bent down to examine their scruffy faces, looking for the flush of fever, the outbreak of pustules, or the gray stillness of death.

Martha Jane Canary (aka Calamity Jane)

Martha Jane knew the risk of close contact with these particular sick men. Settlers and soldiers moving onto the northern plains in 1876 still talked about the terrible smallpox epidemic of 1837. At the first sign of fevers or red lesions, victims were isolated because the contagion spread so quickly—and so fatally. It had literally wiped out whole tribes of Native Americans and killed thousands of fur traders, prospectors, and settlers.

The Indians called it "Rotting Face" because that's exactly what it looked like. Fevers as high as 106 degrees, terrible back pain, a vicious headache that hammered with each heartbeat, chills, nausea, and convulsions marked the onset of the disease. Four days into the illness, the flat, red lesions appeared; then they puffed up and became clear blisters filled with pus that sometimes merged into one gigantic, painful mass.

Smallpox victims were unable to care for themselves and were often dumped into "pest houses" to prevent the spread of the sickness. Twenty-four-year-old Martha Jane Canary knew the symptoms and the fate of those who came into contact with the disease. Yet, she'd volunteered to nurse those in the leaky tents set up outside the town.

She breathed a sigh of relief after studying her patients. None of the men she examined in the cold, damp tent showed those terrifying symptoms. "Hell and Hallelujah," she muttered. One by one, faces turned toward her voice, and crusted, red-rimmed eyes opened. "You boys look worse than grizzly bears with the mange," she cracked. Gesturing toward the covered bucket she'd lugged down from town, Jane announced, "I got venison stew in the bucket."

"You cook it?" asked one man as he struggled up on an elbow. He cast a doubtful glance at the pail.

"Hell, no. But I shot the damn deer just so you don't have to eat no more of that mush you was whinin' about." The fierce frown gave way to a grin. "You boys need to build up your strength. I haven't had a drink or a game since the fever hit, and I'm getting mighty restless."

The men grinned in sympathy. They knew their nurse quite well.

The outbreak of smallpox had decimated the area around Rapid City, Dakota Territory. When troopers at nearby Custer started getting sick by ones and twos, and then by the dozen, Lieutenant Roger Williams, in charge of the encampment, had moved closer to the straggling new settlement. He'd ordered a quarantine area for sick troopers and townspeople before he, too, came down with the fever. The troops were supposed to be guarding against the influx of prospectors until treaties could be made with the Natives, but, by the early spring of 1876, half the company was sick.

Jane was one of the few women willing to brave the "pigsty" camp and the dreaded disease to provide aid for those stricken and unable to care for themselves. Usually newspapers of the time reported her more colorful adventures, but local reporters knew another side of Martha Jane Canary.

"Here were gathered the few women of the camp caring for the sick, and foremost among them was Jane, laboring day and night, scarcely snatching an hour's sleep out of the 24, [*sic*] and always answering each suffering patient's feeble beck or peevish call," recalled the *Black Hills Weekly*.

"It was here that her nickname was coined by the commanding officer of the little camp, who himself was very ill, Lt. Williams, a young West-pointer. He called her 'our angel in calamity . . . Calamity Jane.'"

Buffalo Bill Cody told a different story about the source of Martha Jane Canary's nickname. In 1872, at Goose Creek Camp, near what is now Sheridan, South Dakota, Cody remembered that Jane had established a reputation for daring horsemanship and skill with a rifle.

One day, Bill's story goes, Captain Patrick Egan and some of his men were surrounded by a large band of hostile Natives. They were fighting for their lives when Egan was wounded. He fell from his horse. Jane rode into the melee, snatched up Egan, and raced away. "When he recovered," Buffalo Bill reported, "Captain Egan laughingly spoke of Miss Canary as 'Calamity Jane' and the name has clung to her ever since; so it is that thousands have heard of her, very few have ever heard her real name."

The story changed again in 1903, when a third version of the origin of the nickname was published in the *Weekly Pioneer Times* of Deadwood, South Dakota. The tale is part of an account written three days after Martha Jane Canary's death: "The sobriquet 'Calamity Jane' was given her by Bill Nye during the early seventies when he was editing the Laramie *Boomerang*. She became a rover early in life and traveled over the country with a number of important expeditions, both military and citizen."

Tales of Calamity Jane's exploits abound: She drove the Deadwood stage to town after it had been attacked by Natives; she outwitted bandits during a stint as a pony express rider; she narrowly escaped death with Custer's forces; she rode a big red bull into a saloon; she captured Jack McCall after he shot Wild Bill Hickok in a saloon in Deadwood. Detractors noted that she could cuss with the best, drink as much bad whiskey as the worst, chew tobacco and hit the spittoon every time, and make her bed with anyone who paid for the drinks.

Did the notorious adventurer really risk her own life nursing victims of smallpox, diphtheria, and other plagues?

Her maiden name, she said in her "own story," a pamphlet she later published, was Martha Canary, and she was born in Princeton, Missouri, on May 1, 1852. Her family moved to Virginia City, Montana, in 1865. During the five-month journey, Jane wrote that she spent most of her time hunting with the men of the party, adding "in fact I was at all times with the men when there was excitement and adventures to be had." In her autobiography, she related a version of the naming incident similar to Cody's, as well as a number of other heroic tales.

Her own account of her life indicated that she left an abusive home as a teenager and followed the progress of the construction camps of the Union Pacific Railroad. Others said that was where she got her start as a camp follower. She told the story differently: In 1870, she wrote, she became a scout for General George Custer at Fort Russell, Wyoming. Historians consider that a doubtful claim, in part because she would have been only eighteen years old. If she was with Custer's troops, they say, it is unlikely she was working in any official capacity.

It was with Custer, said Jane, that she "donned the uniform of a soldier." She clearly possessed the necessary skills as well as the courage. Having learned to ride at a very young age and to hunt for the family table as a youngster, Jane clearly was capable of playing more than one role during her time with Custer's troops. There is, however, no official record that she was employed as a scout, or anything else, in Custer's command.

Her own story told it this way: "In spring of 1876, we were ordered north with General Crook to join Gen'ls. Miles, Terry and Custer at Big Horn River. During this march I swam the Platte River at Fort Fetterman as I was the bearer of important dispatches. I had a ninety mile ride to make, being wet and cold I contracted a severe illness and was sent back in Gen. Crook's ambulance to Fort Fetterman where I laid in the hospital for fourteen days."

Writer George Hoshier scoffed at her claims of being a scout. In a long article published in the *Sioux Falls Argus-Leader* of 1906, Hoshier said he first met Jane in 1875 in Cheyenne, Wyoming.

"She did come into the hills with General Crook and wore men's clothes at that time," related Hoshier, "but she was no more of a scout than I was."

She was also, by her own account and those of others who knew her, a bullwhacker, driving trains across the prairies of the Dakota Territory and Wyoming. Driving a "bull train" was not a traditional role for a woman; nor was it a task taken up lightly even by men. Teams of oxen yoked together to form a long train were hitched to freight wagons and guided by a "bullwhacker" armed with a twenty-foot bullwhip. Moving at a slow pace, making seven miles a day was a hard, boring, and monotonous job. Old-timers who knew Jane said that she could cuss with the worst and ply her whip with the best.

Many of those old-timers reported instances when Calamity Jane nursed victims of illness, and the *Deadwood Pioneer* reported she'd taken care of a man "who was stabbed on lower Main Street Wednesday night."

Calamity Jane was also a wife and mother. In her memoirs, she said she married Clinton Burk in 1885 in El Paso, Texas, "as I thought I had traveled through life long enough alone and thought it was about time to take a partner for the rest of my days. We remained in Texas leading a quiet home life." In October 1887, she gave birth to a daughter, "the very image of its father," she wrote, "at least that is what he said, but who has the temper of its mother." Burk, a handsome man who had a job driving a horse cab, later absconded with the proceeds from the business.

Calamity Jane returned to Deadwood with a little girl in October 1895. She hoped to raise enough money to put the child in a good school. The *Black Hills Daily Times* reported the return of "The Fearless Indian Fighter and Rover of the Western Plains," and noted the little girl's presence at Calamity Jane's side. "She has always been known for her friendliness, generosity and happy, cordial manner," the *Times* reporter stated. "It didn't matter to her whether a person was rich or poor, white or black or what their circumstances were, Calamity Jane was just the same to all."

The townsfolk staged a benefit to raise funds for Jane and her daughter, and, with a full purse, Jane reportedly had a few drinks to celebrate; they went to her head, and she would have spent the entire proceeds had not some of the money been rescued by her friends. The daughter, who went unnamed in the accounts written about Jane, was sent to the Sisters' Convent School at Sturgis in South Dakota.

That same year, Jane was offered a contract with the touring entertainment company of Kohl and Middleton. In the East, her reputation had been enhanced by dime novels and lurid stories linking her to Wild Bill Hickok and other infamous characters. That overblown reputation made her a popular attraction. Wearing a suit of fringed buckskin and armed with her customary weaponry, she first appeared in 1896 onstage in Minnesota as the "Famous Woman Scout." The small pamphlet containing the story of her life "as told by herself" was published during that year, and she sold it herself as well.

Never able to walk a straight and narrow path for long, Calamity Jane soon hit the bottle, then clobbered a policeman in Buffalo, New York, and was invited to leave town. Back in the wide open spaces she loved, Jane reportedly worked as a laundress, cook, and nurse. Her reputation for helping the sick was less publicized than that of her carousing, adventuring life, but her willingness to walk into a pest house to care for those unable to help themselves was well established in Deadwood and other areas.

"She was a fine nurse," noted a 1906 story in the *Great Falls Leader*. During the 1878 smallpox epidemic in Deadwood, it was

Calamity Jane who cared for gravely ill miners banished to a little cabin away from town in Spruce Gulch up on the side of a mountain called White Rocks. There was one physician in town, Dr. Babcock, who examined the sick miners, but townsfolk relate that Jane relieved him of their care. Through weeks of toil, she ministered to the eight sick miners, spending her own money for medicine.

One story tells that she, being quarantined as well, would hurry to the head of the gulch and call down to the men working that stream below that she needed supplies. They would go to town and fill the order. Jane would then hoist up the pack by rope. Despite her efforts, three of the sick men died. She wrapped them in a blanket, yelled to the miners to dig a hole, and then lowered the bodies for burial. During the long weeks of the epidemic, Jane worked ceaselessly, and Deadwood never forgot.

One unnamed correspondent quoted an account of the "terrible scourge of smallpox among the miners and people of Deadwood. Hundreds were prostrate upon their rude beds and most people were afraid to go near them. Women were few to be had and they, too, were in terror of their lives. In the house of terror and death, there came to the front a willing volunteer, the mule-skinning, bull whacking and rough, roving woman from the depths—Calamity Jane." The handwritten pages contained in the collection of materials of the South Dakota Historical Society balance the hard-drinking, hard-living Calamity Jane against the generous and dedicated nurse also known as Calamity Jane.

"How often amid the snows of winter did this woman find her way to a lonely cabin of a miner who was suffering from the disease of those times and who felt sorely the need of food and medicine?" recalled an account in the *Pioneer Times* in 1906. "When the history of this country is written too much cannot be said of the results of this woman's labors."

She performed the same selfless service in Pierre, South Dakota, during an epidemic in which a family of settlers had been virtually abandoned for dread of the "black diphtheria." She reportedly spent most of the little money she had on medicines for the family and stayed with them until they could care for themselves.

In another instance, a Deadwood old-timer reported that she had nursed his sister, ill with mountain fever. Wearing a dress and eschewing tobacco and drink for the duration, Jane faithfully discharged her duties as nurse until the lady recovered, then lit out for the nearest saloon to quench a prodigious thirst.

When Jane became ill at fifty, she was living at the Calloway Hotel in Terry, South Dakota. The *Pioneer Times* reported that she'd arrived ill in Terry from Spearfish, South Dakota, and she'd mentioned to friends that she expected to be "cashing in" any day. She died of pneumonia August 1, 1903, and was taken back to Deadwood by her friends. She was buried there at the Mount Moriah Cemetery.

Even in death, Calamity Jane's legend grew. Stories were told that she and Wild Bill Hickok had had a love affair that died when he was shot as he sat at a gaming table in a Deadwood saloon. Some stories add she chased down the shooter, Jack McCall. Calamity's own story said she'd left her gun hanging on a bedpost and, having located McCall in a butcher shop, grabbed a meat cleaver and made him surrender. Most accounts claim McCall was captured by many local citizens who gave chase after the shooting.

Jane said she and Hickock were just friends, but they had arrived in Deadwood together in 1876 and were seen occasionally together. Two such legendary figures appearing in the same Wild West town at the same time almost guaranteed that a fantasy romance between the two would be created. Dime novels, books, and movies have embroidered the truth from the time McCall fired the fatal bullet and Hickock slumped over the cards he held. Even the cards became part of the legend—the famous "Dead Man's Hand" of aces and eights.

When she died twenty-seven years later, one newspaper reported that Jane's "last request" was to be buried beside the grave of her former husband, William Hickok. There was absolutely no truth to the claim they were married. Nevertheless, Martha Jane Canary was buried in the same Deadwood cemetery as Wild Bill, adding another layer of gilding to the legend of Calamity Jane.

CHAPTER 12

Juliet Fish Nichols

Lighthouse Keeper

Just off Fort Point are several rocks that are a terror to mariners and on which many a good ship has laid her bones. The currents here, right in the jaws of the entrance to the harbor, are very strong and irregular, and in case of fog the rocks are extremely dangerous.
—SAN FRANCISCO CHRONICLE, NOVEMBER 10, 1895

THICK, DAMP, AND COLD FOG PRESSED AGAINST THE WINDOWS OF the small house at Point Knox, condensed in a muted bronze gleam on the huge bell, slipped clammy fingers inside the cloak of the woman shivering on the small platform. Waves splashed and foamed against the rocks far below the wet planks where Juliet Fish Nichols listened tensely for the creak of rigging or the dull thunder of a steamship's engine. She hoped she heard something before she saw it because any ship close enough to see was doomed.

Automatically, her throbbing arm lifted, and she rapped the small hammer twice against the side of the three-thousand-pound bell. Fifteen seconds later, she struck the bell again. Then, after counting off another fifteen seconds, she elevated the hammer and

Juliet Fish Nichols, *San Francisco Chronicle*, June 15, 1890

banged twice more on the great bell. Again and again, eight times each minute, Juliet lifted her aching arm and rang the bell, warning ships away from Angel Island in fogbound San Francisco Bay.

At least four ships were due in port that first week of July 1906: the *Capac*, *City of Topeka*, and *Sea Foam*, all of which plied the California coast, as well as the transpacific steamer *Mongolia* loaded with passengers from the Far East. Unfortunately, the crystal-clear atmosphere of July 1 had deteriorated rapidly in the following few days. Visibility was often no more than a few yards. Impenetrable fog concealed every landmark.

Juliet had seen the annual summer phenomenon many times, but this year the job of warning approaching ships away was doubly important. Rebuilding was in full swing following the great 1906 earthquake. The already hectic harbor was a mad scramble of activity with hundreds of ships attempting to navigate the bay's treacherous currents, escape ship-eating rocks, and find their way through heavy fog. The lighthouses, fog sirens, and bells were critically important.

Juliet stood on the small platform with a hammer in hand because, once again, the Gamewell Fire Alarm Number 3 clockworks, which powered the mechanism that rang the Angel Island bell, had quit working. During a brief lifting of the fog, Juliet had sent a telegram to the lighthouse engineer and then serviced the small, stationary red light on the southwest corner of the station. Because the light was intended for fair nights and not thick fog, it would be virtually useless as a warning.

In the distance, she heard the intermittent signals of foghorns at various locations on San Francisco Bay. She hoped those warnings would stop any ships from proceeding until the fog lifted. Navigation was always tricky against treacherous currents and strong tides. In a thick fog, Angel Island, Alcatraz Island, and Yerba Buena were nearly invisible. There was no one but herself to warn mariners away from the narrow channel between Angel Island and Sausalito, where more than one ship had gone to a watery grave.

Juliet straightened with a snap at a familiar sound. She gripped the hammer tightly and peered into the clammy gray wall before her. A faint swish and creak, the sound of voices, and, suddenly, the masts of a sailing vessel coalesced from the mist. With a shout, she cracked a clamorous warning against the bell, creating a deafening din. Yells of alarm from unseen sailors carried across the choppy waters. Muscles burned as she hammered the bell until the masts disappeared into the mist.

With her heart beating high and hard, she listened for the agonizing crash that would signal the end for the ship whose name she didn't know. Minutes later her arm fell to her side, cramped fingers frozen to the handle of the hammer. Silence, blessed silence, instead of the shrieks of drowning men. With a shuddering sigh, she unclamped her fingers, changed hands, and again took up the rhythm of the Angel Island bell: two beats every fifteen seconds.

The next morning, the thick blanket lifted, and a wave of ships entered the bay from the Pacific; ferries once again carried passengers to and fro, and the merchant ships carrying summer produce from Stockton and Sacramento bustled into port. "Mr. Burt came on July 3rd at 10 a.m. and made slight repairs," Juliet wrote in a report to the lighthouse inspector. "Meanwhile I had struck the bell by hand for twenty (20) hours and thirty-five (35) minutes, until the fog lifted."

That evening the fog once more crept through the low points of the western hills of San Francisco and poured silently across the bay. Juliet slept uneasily, rising every two hours to wind the mechanism that automatically rang the bell. Her arms ached from the hours beating the bell with the hammer the day before, but there was little rest that night, either, because the heavy clockworks took twenty minutes to rewind.

"On the night of July 3rd, 1906, the machinery worked badly, striking irregularly," Juliet reported. The next day a fog bank menaced the city, held back by its famous steep hills. By seven o'clock that evening, the battle was lost, and the bay was blanketed in dense fog. "On the fourth of July the machinery went to pieces, the great tension bar broke in two and I could not disconnect the hammer to strike by hand. I stood all night on the platform outside and struck the bell with a nail hammer with all my might. The fog was dense, with heavy mist, almost rain." In the July 5 report that she wrote about the preceding three days, Juliet noted that the machinist from the office of the lighthouse engineer, located in San Francisco, had finally arrived and replaced the tension bar just as she was writing the account.

By the foggy summer of 1906, Juliet had served as keeper of the Angel Island station for four years. She had the satisfaction of knowing that her efforts were important to the crew and passengers whom made it safely to port, but she also had the frustration of dealing with a piece of equipment that became more unreliable the more she needed it. Because of the intense vibration and the constant tension on the clockworks that regulated the heavy sledgehammer that rang the bell, the mechanism was prone to fail during long periods of foggy weather.

San Francisco had a legendary reputation as one of the foggiest harbors in the nation. Although it was often foggy in winter, the peculiar phenomenon of heavy summer fog made bells and sirens critical to nautical safety. In her first few years as keeper of the light, she'd seen more foggy days in summer than ever before in her life.

The daughter of an army physician, Dr. Melancthon Fish, Juliet was born in China in 1859. Her mother died giving birth to her, and her mother's sister, Emily, ventured to the Orient to care for her niece. Emily later married Juliet's father. After returning to California from China, where Dr. Fish had served as vice consul of Shanghai, the family became prominent in the Bay Area. Dr. Fish taught university-level classes, and he, his wife, and daughter were active in the social life of Oakland, across the bay from San Francisco.

Juliet's wedding to Commander Henry Nichols in 1888 was prominently featured in San Francisco's *Daily Morning Call*. Juliet was thirty years old, and Henry was forty-five. The newspaper reported that the bride had graduated from Mills College and the groom had successfully commanded two ships prior to their wedding day. The floral counterpart of a full-rigged vessel was part of the wedding decorations, and they were married under an archway of white chrysanthemums set up in the bay window of her father's Oakland home.

Henry was, at that time, working for the Coast and Geodetic Survey and for several years spent summers mapping in Alaska. Juliet lived in "a handsome residence on Ninth Avenue and Twenty-third Street—which was her bridal gift from her father," reported the *Call* in 1890. Henry later was appointed superintendent of the Twelfth Lighthouse District, which covered the California coast.

When Dr. Fish died, Henry appointed his mother-in-law, Emily, to the light keeper's position at Point Pinos on the Monterey Peninsula. Emily Fish was one of the few women not directly related to a male light keeper to serve in such a critical position. Little did Juliet dream that she, too, would be widowed a few years later and that she would accept a similar position. In 1902, two years after her husband's death in the Philippines while serving in the Spanish-American War, Juliet was given the post of lighthouse keeper at Angel Island.

She lived there alone. The small station was isolated, accessible only by boat and a long, steep, wooden stairway. The little house perched precariously on a rocky outcropping at the western edge of the island. The house was remodeled after Juliet took over. The rear porch was enclosed and became the kitchen; the former kitchen became the living room, and the pantry became a bathroom and water closet with stationary washtubs. A shed had been built for wood and coal needed for heating and cooking.

The small house sat in a thirty-by-thirty-foot plot of rocky dirt, but Juliet managed to cultivate two small flower beds there. Access to the outside world required a long climb up the staircase perched on the steep granite bluff, then a trek across the military reservation on the island, for which she needed an official pass. From there she caught a government steamer to take her to town to buy supplies, see a doctor, or pay a visit to a friend.

In a 1903 letter to the Lighthouse Board, Commander J. B. Milton asked that the keeper be permitted to purchase supplies from the Subsistence Department of the army at Angel Island. "Mrs. Nichols has related to me that during the last winter she was, on several occasions, in a bad way for provisions, owning to the fact that she is alone, being unable to send to the city and of course could not leave the station herself."

Commander Milton pointed out that the "station is not allowed a ration and the salary is so small that the Keeper is unable to pay an assistant." Later that year, permission was granted to allow Juliet to purchase "subsistence stores" subject to several conditions, including a 10 percent surcharge and only if the post commander decided the army could spare the goods.

In 1905, Commander W. P. Day requested a pay increase for Juliet. "There is only one keeper at this station, and a woman at that, and she has been up on one occasion 83 [*sic*] consecutive hours and obliged to strike the bell by hand a considerable part of that time." Milton believed the station should have assistance but acknowledged the difficulties.

"As this station is built on a small detached rock, the quarters are constricted; I would therefore respectfully recommend an increase in salary of the present keeper from $600 to $750 per annum, on condition that she employs a servant to assist her in her duties as Keeper." She would, in effect, earn about $63 a month—but to get the raise, part of it would have to be spent on wages for a helper.

Juliet's raise was approved, although there is no record that she ever hired help. Her new salary was less than the Alcatraz keeper's $800 annual pay, and the Alcatraz keeper was assigned two assistants whom were paid $500 a year each by the Lighthouse Board, not the keeper.

Alcatraz and Angel Island were equally important in protecting shipping in the bay. Mid-nineteenth-century news accounts, editorials, and letters to the Corps of Engineers show that the lack of a fog signal at Angel Island had been a problem for years. On the other hand, having an unreliable signal was considered almost a worse problem.

"A fog signal, to answer all the requirements, must not only be very powerful, very efficient, and very simple, but it must be very reliable; for it is better to have none at all than one that stops frequently because [it's] out for repairs," noted the *Alta California* newspaper in January 1869.

Juliet was only the second keeper at Angel Island. It had taken years of constant requests before the bell station was finally approved. Requests had repeatedly been made for a signal on the island, located just past the entrance to the bay. For years, the heavy fogs and tidal rips had taken a toll on shipping. The loss of ships and crew and the wealth that sank to the bottom of the bay with each shipwreck had merchants and politicians lobbying for help. One report from June 2, 1854, showed that three steamships alone had carried more than two million dollars in "treasure" the day before. The loss of such cargoes weighed heavily in the long-delayed decision to install a fog signal at Angel Island.

More than fifteen years of shipping disasters and much political pressure bore fruit in 1885 when $4,500 was appropriated to put a fog bell at Point Knox on the western side of Angel Island. Construction was not an easy job. The first attempts to build the station were nearing completion in 1886 when a violent storm and landslide ripped away the trail and the wooden steps necessary to scale the steep cliff. Because so many ships passed through the narrow channel between Point Knox and Sausalito and because the strong tides and rocky outcroppings were so dangerous, more money was appropriated to rebuild. In 1887, the station was finally activated.

The keeper's quarters and signal house were connected to the top of the steep hillside by a wooden stairway with 151 steps. Water was delivered via a pipeline from the army post on the other side of the island. In the three years after the station went into operation, landslides twice took out the stairs, the water line, and a small storage building. The clockwork mechanism that automatically ran the bell broke down regularly—all this before Juliet took on the job at the Point Knox station. Any keeper there was at the mercy of the elements.

———

The summer of 1906 was particularly foggy, and the bell's mechanism was extremely unreliable. It was a year of trials for San

Francisco. On April 18, Juliet helplessly watched through binoculars as the bustling city shuddered and tumbled and then burst into flames. Her own station on the island had survived the massive earthquake without mishap, but across the bay the city became a raging inferno. Unable to communicate with the outside world for hours, she worried about the only living member of her family—her stepmother, Emily, keeper of the Point Pinos light. Two days later, she learned that Emily was safe and the Point Pinos lighthouse had survived the terrible earthquake with only minor damage.

Towns as far as one hundred miles away had suffered damage in the quake. Wreckage of roads and rail systems hampered relief efforts, but ships carrying badly needed supplies kept the bay's shipping lanes busier than ever. All that spring and early summer, Juliet stayed vigilant, lighting the small red lamp that marked Angel Island and winding the machinery that kept the bell going until it gave out that memorable day three months after the 1906 quake.

Juliet received a commendation from the commissioner of lighthouses for the twenty-hour marathon with her trusty hammer. It might have been more rewarding if they had also replaced the machinery that automatically struck the bell. She wrote numerous letters, sent telegrams, and reported many more instances when her hammer and her arm were the only warnings for ships negotiating the hazardous rocks in the fogbound bay.

Her log for November 19, 1908, recorded dense fog all night and the breaking of a steel pin in the mechanism that disabled the bell. Once again, she grabbed her hammer and stood outside banging it twice every fifteen seconds for more than four hours. Forty-five minutes after the fog lifted, she reported the incident by telegraph, but at 10:00 a.m. the fog settled in again, and she rang the bell by hand for another hour. Similar reports are repeated every year in the log Juliet kept until she retired. She turned the station over to her replacement, Peter Admiral, on November 19, 1914.

Admiral's first year was a busy one, to say the least. During that year, Juliet usually saw sunshine break through the morning fog at her home in Oakland, but the station she'd left on Angel Island was frequently immersed in the mist. The *San Francisco Lightship* reported 2,145 hours of fog that year, and in 1916 the lightship was fogbound for 2,221 hours, or about 25 percent of the year. Juliet's replacement had just as much trouble with the fog bell.

Juliet lived quietly in Oakland to the age of eighty-eight. The Angel Island fog bell was automated in the 1960s, and the keeper vacated the quarters on the rocky point. The house was burned to the ground in 1963. The bell remained in place for years, its dulled sides showing the marks of a hammer wielded by one valiant woman.

CHAPTER 13

Pauline Cushman

Spy of the Cumberland

We have now among us one of those heroic women, whose glorious courage and unflinching personal sacrifice have given a tinge of the olden times romances to the somber annual of our terrible Civil War.

—ANNOUNCEMENT LISTED IN THE *JANESVILLE WEEKLY GAZETTE* ABOUT PAULINE CUSHMAN'S ARRIVAL IN WISCONSIN, JUNE 24, 1864

AMONG THE EXHIBITS ON DISPLAY AT P. T. BARNUM'S AMERICAN Theatre in New York City during the summer of 1864 was an actress and patriot of the Union army named Pauline Cushman. Billed as the "Spy of Cumberland," the celebrated thespian was dressed in the complete uniform of an infantry man, including a saber, a crimson, silk sash, and a forage cap. Her hair under the cap was disheveled, shoulder-length, and curly. She sported a mustache, thin, but unmistakable above her upper lip, and below the lip was a dark tuft of hair. The makeup and overall look was so convincing that unless otherwise notified ticket buyers had no idea the man was really a woman.

Pauline Cushman appeared on stage in the lecture room at P. T. Barnum's American Theatre from June 6, 1864, to July 9, 1864. She offered a patriotic presentation to more than twenty thousand people in a single month. According to the advertisement issued by P. T. Barnam about Pauline's engagement, "she was the modern American model of the renowned 'Joan of Arc.'"

"Miss Pauline Cushman, the Union scout and spy, who under orders from General Rosecrans, passed through enemy lines and accomplished such wonders for the Army of the Cumberland while she was engaged in the secret service of the United States," the July 6, 1864, edition of the *Charleston Mercury* read. "Every father and mother who have a son in the Union Army; every child who has learned to love its country and call on heaven to bless its present struggle and preserve its nationality, will rejoice at this opportunity of listening to 'thoughts that breathe and words that burn,' as they fall from the lips of this high-souled, gallant girl, who, in her determination to serve her country, risked her inestimable precious life, and was rescued from a Rebel prison, where by order of the notorious General Bragg, she lay wounded and languishing with sickness, UNDER SENTENCE OF DEATH!

"Those who would avoid the crowd should bear in mind that the most pleasant time to hear this heroic lady recount, in her fervid language, her adventure, is at ELEVEN O'CLOCK IN THE MORNING, on which the lecture room is thrown open without any extra charge. The public's obedient servant, P. T. Barnum."

Pauline Cushman was born Harriet Pauline Wood on June 10, 1833, in the old French section of New Orleans, Louisiana. Her father was a Spanish businessman and political refugee; her mother, a beautiful French girl of some social prominence. When Pauline was ten years old her father moved his family to the wilderness of Michigan. It was there that the Chippewa Indian children were

Pauline's playmates. They taught her to paddle a canoe and ride a pony. They called her "Laughing Breeze," and the older women taught her how to cook and sew.

At the age of eighteen, Pauline ran away from home to New York City. She soon got an audition before Thomas Placide, the manager of the New Orleans Varieties theater, who was in New York recruiting performers for his company. He gave Pauline a minor role in a popular show entitled *New Orleans*. Pauline's gypsy-like beauty captivated audiences from the start and she went far in the entertainment world. Her name was changed to Cushman, a name she held all her life even through three marriages.

Pauline toured the theatrical circuits from New York to San Francisco. She shared the stage with such infamous entertainers as Lola Montez and Adah Menken. Pauline appeared in such popular plays as *Much Ado About Nothing*, *Romeo and Juliet*, and *Mazeppa*. Theatergoers from coast to coast thought she was a clever comedian able to speak and sing to the audiences' satisfaction. In *Mazeppa*, a play based on a poem by Lord Byron about a lovesick equestrian who has an affair with a countess and is then punished for leading the maiden astray, Pauline portrayed Mazeppa. She was the first woman to play a male role on the American stage. Her performance was praised as a daring innovation.

The thrill of the footlights did not satisfy the adventurous actress, however. In 1863, the Civil War was raging fiercely when Pauline arrived in Louisville, Kentucky, to appear in another production of *Mazeppa*. As usual a throng of admirers gathered at the Wood's Playhouse to see the well-known performer and engage her in conversation about her career. Among those at the scene were a number of paroled Rebel officers. Upon introducing themselves to Pauline, they asked if she would do something for them. "They proposed at first laughingly, and then seriously, to make me a present of $300, if during my performance I would make a certain toast," the actress remembered in the biography *Life of Pauline Cushman: The Celebrated Union Spy and Scout.* The Rebel soldiers wanted her to say, "Here's to Jeff Davis and the southern Confederacy, may the south always maintain her honor and her rights." Shocked at the proposition Pauline responded, "But good gracious, gentlemen! I should be locked up in jail if I were to attempt anything of that kind." The men repeated the request and promised to take care of everything.

Pauline politely excused herself from the gathering and hurried to meet with Colonel Orlando Moore, a Union Provost Marshal she had been introduced to earlier in the day. After a serious conversation, Colonel Moore asked that she honor the request. "Of course," the colonel assured her, "I know that you would not feel it; if I were not sure of that, I should arrest you immediately; but if you are willing to serve our country, do this."

"Willing to serve my country," she responded sincerely, "I would die for it!"

"Die for it if need be; if not live for it," Colonel Moore continued. "If you will only do this, you can do more real service than a regiment of men."

Before Pauline had taken the stage in early April 1863, Colonel Moore had persuaded her to enter the secret service of the Union.

According to the June 24, 1864, edition of the *Janesville Weekly Gazette*, the Wood's Theatre was packed the night Pauline offered the toast to Jefferson Davis. "The incident fell upon the multitude like a thunder clap," the *Janesville Weekly Gazette* article read, "confusing and mortifying all loyal persons present, and highly delighting their neighbors. This of course led to her mock arrest and dismissal from the theatre. Speedily released, she next repaired to Nashville, and while there engaged at the new theatre it was

Major Pauline Cushman, the Union Spy of the Cumberland

suggested to her by Colonel W. Truesdail the chief of army police to make a little excursion to the headquarters of the Confederate General Bragg. This idea fully coinciding with her own innate love of wild and dashing adventures, and an excellent pretext being availed in the fact that she had a brother in the service, she willingly undertook the expedition, after having solemnly accepted the following oath.

"I, Pauline Cushman, do solemnly swear that I will bear true allegiance and fidelity to the government of the United State of America, and that I will faithfully serve the same during the time I am employed in the service of the Army of the Cumberland, to the best of my knowledge and ability; that I will observe and obey all the instructions which may be given me; that I will in no manner or form convey or give any information to the enemies of the government of the United States which will be advantage to them, or injury to the Federal cause, so help me God.

"The Colonel then gave her a series of very minute, solemn and impressive instructions for her guidance, and she set forth as a refugee and victim of northern tyranny."

Nashville was a vast Southern-aide society with treasonous goals—aiding and passing information to the enemy. Orders had been given by General Braxton Bragg that since few people could be trusted not to be spies—no man was allowed to leave Nashville without leave or he would be put on a block and shot.

On May 27, 1863, Colonel Truesdail gave Pauline instructions to leave town with a number of other women who were Southern sympathizers. Of course, Pauline was only pretending to be a Southern sympathizer to gain access to Confederate headquarters in the field. Not only was she posing as a victim of the Union army dismissed from town, but she had plans to infiltrate the Rebel lines by claiming to look for her brother, who was a Rebel soldier under

General Bragg. She was eventually captured by the Rebel army inside their lines and escorted to General Bragg.

On the way for Pauline to be delivered to the general, Rebel soldiers stopped at a hotel in Shelbyville for food and supplies. The soldiers had important plans and drawings of defense fortifications with them. Using her talent and charm, Pauline managed to distract the men long enough for her to steal the important documents and smuggle them out to a female farmer and fellow spy who took the material to Colonel Truesdail.

Not only did Pauline hijack key documents but she made sketches of the fortifications, troop location, and troop numbers. She transferred copies of the information to Union loyalists who got the intelligence to the appropriate people. When there was no one to take the secret dispatches or mail she acquired to Colonel Truesdail safely, she stole unlisted personnels' clothing and dressed like a man and made her way to the area where she knew the Union forces would be waiting.

The best of fortune followed Pauline during her monthlong adventure as a spy. Her dashing beauty had disarmed the severest of her foes. The versatile actress was ultimately able to acquire crucial reports about the size, strength, and deployment of General Bragg's troops. Those reports revealed that General Bragg was a close military advisor to the confederal President Jefferson Davis. The information Pauline secured resulted in Southern troops being outmaneuvered in the Tullahoma Campaign and the Union pushing the Rebels out of Chattanooga, Tennessee.

By the end of June 1863, good luck seemed to have deserted Pauline. She was arrested in the dead of night by Rebel scouts who suspected she might be a spy after she was seen sneaking around a Confederate picket post near Franklin. General John Hunt Morgan and three Rebel scouts tracked Pauline to a farm where she had taken refuge. She had been exploring the area to ascertain the position and strength of the Rebel troops after their retreat from Chattanooga. Pauline was searched and key documents were found hidden in a secret compartment in her shoe.

The June 24, 1864, edition of the *Janesville Weekly Gazette* reported that General John Hunt Morgan was a "renowned guerrilla chieftain who was more than pleased to escort Pauline to the quarters of General Nathan Bedford Forrest." While en route to the distinguished officer, General Morgan became enthralled with Pauline's beauty. "Johnnie manifested all the gallantry that usually distinguishes such a man in the presence of the fair and offered the beautiful Pauline all his friendship; a magnificent diamond ring and a silver mounted revolver as keepsakes and urged her to become his aide-de-camp as soon as she should be released," the *Janesville Weekly Gazette* article continued.

General Forrest was not at all pleased to see Pauline in his camp. He didn't smile when he was introduced to her, nor did he shake her hand. He was disgusted to meet a spy. He motioned for her to sit down and she complied. "I've been looking for spies like you for a long time, but I've got you now and intend to hold you," General Forrest told Pauline. "You have been here before. You know all the roads, bride-paths and hog-paths."

"That's false," Pauline responded, "I've never been here and would like to send a bullet through the man mean enough to make the charge."

General Forrest gazed at her with amusement while she continued. "Well, you're made of good fighting stuff if you're a woman."

"I got my visit south as a poor refugee expelled from the Union lines on account of strong southern feeling," and she accounted most adroitly for the absence of her baggage, stating that she had been deprived of all by Colonel Truesdail. The general questioned her as to her plans for the future in the South, the position and resources of the Union army.

Pauline managed to address all of Forrest's queries to his satisfaction. He informed her that he was going to hand her over to the Confederate Provost Marshal General Colonel McKinstry. Forrest told her that the general was a "humane and just man" who would investigate the serious charges against her and get at the truth.

The idea of being sent to the Provost Marshal did not frighten Pauline. She maintained her strong Confederate loyalty. She was dispatched to Rebel headquarters at Shelbyville. Before she was escorted away, Johnnie Morgan offered her his good wishes.

"Goodbye! I hope we shall meet again where we can have something better than cornbread baked in ashes and rotgut whisky at fifteen dollars per quart." Her parting song as she rode away was the well-known ballad "Trust in Luck."

Once Pauline and the men guarding her made it to Shelbyville, she was immediately taken to General Bragg. She sat down in a chair opposite the officer, and he began to question her extensively.

"I am of French and Spanish descent," Pauline offered.

"Where were you born," he pressed.

"In New Orleans," she replied.

"Your speech favors a Yankee twang."

"Well, I'm an actress and have been playing Yankee parts so long that I suppose I've caught the twang." She then went on to narrate the history of her fighting qualities from the woman she admired the most, "my own brave mother."

"But to the point," the general offered. "You have important papers in your possession and if they prove you to be a spy, nothing can save you from a little hemp."

She carelessly replied, "Well go on and root the whole thing up, if you like."

Picking up a basket of letters, he in turn, said, "By sending out spies I know everything that goes on at the Yankee headquarters better than their own clerks there!"

"But if I'm found guilty," Pauline inquired, "what will you do with me?"

"You will surely be hanged."

"General, come now! I don't think I'd be either useful or ornamental dangling at the end of a rope. If I must die, let me choose the method of my death."

"I cannot promise that because you might prefer a natural mode of exit."

"No, if I must perish, let me be shot, for that would not hurt me so much."

"Where did you get the pistol you had in your possession when you were recaptured at Baum's house?"

"I took it from a house where we stopped at Hillsboro. It belonged to a wounded soldier."

"What did you intend to do with it?"

"As the scouts had left me and the Union army was reported to be near, I took it for self-defense."

At the conclusion of the questioning, Pauline was taken from General Bragg to the Provost Marshal's office, where she met Colonel Alexander McKinstry. The colonel asked her a number of his own questions, including queries about the papers and sketches found in the secret compartment in her shoe. She did not have a satisfactory answer for the papers and sketches. She was then escorted to a private house near the Duck River close to Shelbyville, where she was locked in and placed under guard.

On June 26, 1863, Pauline became extremely ill with typhoid fever and wasn't able to get out of bed for more than a week. While she was convalescing she was informed by an officer that a court-martial board had been assembled and investigated her case. Colonel McKinstry delivered the news of the board's decision. They determined that Pauline was a spy, and she was sentenced to death.

She grew even more ill in the passing days. In addition to suffering from typhoid, she was now overcome with worry over the idea of being hanged. According to the biography *Life of Pauline Cushman: The Celebrated Union Spy and Scout*, "An agony of mind, worse than all these, was what consumed her brain and wasted her fair form . . . Her health seemed to have received a shock from which it is probable it will never fully recover. Fits of deep depression would seize her, and great fears would steal unconsciously down her marble-like features."

On June 28, 1863, Pauline was transported from the home where she was being held prisoner and hurried through the battle lines of Shelbyville to Nashville. She continued to struggle with poor health that kept her from being able to get around on her own. She was kept under constant watch by the Confederates during her incarceration in Nashville. She was still on her sickbed in late September 1863 when the Union army broke through enemy lines and rescued her.

Pauline returned to Louisville once her health improved. According to the December 2, 1863, edition of the *Louisville Journal*, residents of the area were thrilled that the actress-turned-soldier had come back. "This distinguished lady arrived in our city yesterday," the article boasted. "She will be heartily welcomed by her friends and her admirers in this place. The career of this lady, since she left our city, has been one of the wildest romances, and perhaps the most eventful of all heroines who have figured in this war."

In recognition of her service and value to the Union forces, President Abraham Lincoln and General James Garfield conferred upon her the rank of major.

After the war Pauline returned to the stage and traveled throughout the West delivering lectures in various cities for the benefit of charitable institutions. Her admirers would cheer and fire their guns into the ceiling. She played to the wildest audiences on the whole frontier.

In 1879 in San Gabrielle, California, she met and married her third husband, Jeremiah Fryer. They moved to Casa Grande, where south of the Southern Pacific railroad terminal they put in a hotel and livery stable. One of Pauline's principal activities during her life in the Southwest was providing prospectors with money or other assistance to start their enterprise. According to the March 24, 1941, edition of the *Arizona Republic*, Pauline helped numerous hopeful prospectors. "It is legendary that men who were looking for all kinds of metals under almost every condition, principally adverse, knew that when their luck ran low they could get a stake from Pauline Cushman," the *Arizona Republic* article noted. "These grubstakes largely were charity, though legend has it that a few paid Miss Cushman well for her faith and timely assistance."

Several newspaper accounts from 1893 report that Pauline and her husband had a problem with alcohol. Hard drinking was a part of the lives of many people with whom Pauline and Jeremiah came in contact, and the saloon the couple owned was always fully stocked. Pauline's excessive drinking often led to trouble. The August 20, 1975, edition of the *Casa Grande Dispatch* reported a tale about Pauline's drinking woes that had been told many times. "One morning a muleteer was throwing the harness on his mules when Pauline spotted one with raw shoulders from an ill-fitting collar," the article read. "She told him to cut the mule out and he told her to go to hell. So she aimed a 30-30 at his head and started counting. He changed his mind and cut the mule out."

The adverse effect alcohol had on Pauline oftentimes gave her the courage to take on Jeremiah's mistresses. She would announce to the neighborhood her feelings about the "harlots" keeping time with her husband and threaten to "beat the women senseless if they didn't stay away from her man." It was not uncommon for Casa Grande residents to witness a fistfight between Pauline and one of Jeremiah's girlfriends.

In the mid-1880s, Pauline and Jeremiah moved to Florence, Arizona, where Jeremiah was elected the Pinal County sheriff. On November 15, 1881, Pauline presented Jeremiah with a daughter she named Emma. Jeremiah, who traveled a great deal and was away from home for long periods at a time, was not aware he was going to be a father. Pauline, too, had been out of town, and when she returned with the child in her arms she happily told her husband the news that the baby was theirs.

Jeremiah was indeed the father, but Pauline was not the infant's mother. Pauline learned of a woman who was going to have her husband's child and arranged to raise the little girl named Emma as her own. The unwed baby's mother agreed to the plan in order to escape social stigma.

Emma struggled with a number of health issues, including a weak heart, and she died on April 17, 1888. When Jeremiah learned the truth about his daughter's real mother the two separated. Pauline moved to the San Francisco area and Jeremiah stayed behind in Arizona and raised the son he had with a woman named Rita Rodriguez. Pauline and Jeremiah never divorced.

Pauline was living in Oakland in 1893 when the government approved a request for her to receive a pension for her service during the Civil War. The pension amount was a mere eight dollars a month. Time and great loss had taken a toll on Pauline's already fragile health, and a suggestion was made that she should move to the Crocker's Old People's Home in San Francisco. Among Pauline's physical ills were sciatica in her knees, heart problems, and rheumatic pains. She used opiates, prescribed by her doctors to deal with the pain. Pauline refused to move into the home, choosing instead to take a room at a boardinghouse where the owner could care for her.

On Saturday, December 2, 1893, the owner of the boardinghouse where Pauline was living discovered the former spy lying on the floor in her room near death. The doctors were called to the scene and after a quick examination determined that Pauline had overdosed on morphine. They tried to revive her but were unable to save her life.

News of the courageous Union spy's death spread quickly. Newspaper articles from the *San Francisco Call* to the *New York Sun* reported on Pauline's demise. "The state of absolute poverty in which 'Major' Cushman died rendered it possible that she would be interred as a pauper in the Potter's field," the December 5, 1893, edition of the *San Francisco Call* noted. "Patriotic citizens have come forward to prevent this indignity being offered to one whose love of country made her risk so much in its cause.

"The Grand Army of the Republic has undertaken the arrangements for the major's internment. Her body was embalmed yesterday and placed in a handsome cloth-covered casket donated as a tribute of admiration by the undertaker from whose parlor the funeral will take place. The burial services will be conducted tomorrow in the undertaker's parlor.

"An inquest was held yesterday on Pauline Cushman Fryer's body. The jury returned a verdict that Mrs. Fryer's death was caused by an overdose of morphine taken without suicidal intent and to relieve pain."

Pauline Cushman was buried at the San Francisco National Cemetery. She was sixty years old when she passed away.

BIBLIOGRAPHY

CHAPTER 1: FRANCITA ALAVEZ

Barnard, Joseph. *Dr. J. H. Barnard's Journal.* Texas State Archives, 1912.

Boyle, Andrew A. "Reminiscences of the Texas Revolution." *Southwestern Historical Quarterly Online* 13, no. 4. https://tshaonline.org/shqonline.

Brown, John Henry. *History of Texas from 1685 to 1892.* St. Louis: Daniell, 1892.

Corner, William. "John Crittenden Duval: The Last Survivor of the Goliad Massacre." *Southwestern Historical Quarterly Online* 1, no. 1. https://tshaonline.org/shqonline.

Harbert, Davenport. "The Angel of Goliad." Sons of DeWitt Colony Texas, 1997.

Ornish, Natalie. *Ehrenberg: Goliad Survivor. Old West Explorer.* Dallas: Texas Heritage Press, 1997.

Orozco, Cynthia E. "O'SHEA, MARIA ELENA ZAMORA." *Handbook of Texas Online*: www.tshaonline.org/handbook/online/article/fors21. Austin: Texas State Historical Association, 1992.

Perry, Carmen, editor and translator. *With Santa Anna in Texas: A Personal Narrative of the Revolution* by Jose de la Pena. College Station: Texas A&M University Press, 1997.

Roell, Craig H. *Remember Goliad! A History of La Bahia.* Austin: Texas State Historical Association, 1994.

Shackelford, Jack. "Alavez, Francita. Goliad Massacre." *Handbook of Texas Online*: www.tamu.edu/faculty/ccbn.

Washington, Lewis. "Fannin and His Command." Austin: *Georgia Citizen, Texas State Gazette*, 1853.

From the Collection of the Barker State History Center, Texas:
Commercial Bulletin, June 25, 1836.
Dallas News, March 15, 1936.
Natchez Courier, August 23, 1836.
New Orleans Bee, no date.
Southern Messenger, March 15, 1836.
Telegraph and Public Register, August 16, 1836.

CHAPTER 2: JUANA NAVARRO ALSBURY

Alsbury, Juana Gertrudis Navarro. *Handbook of Texas Online*: https://tshaonline.org/handbook/online.

Broadside, October 2, 1835. Austin: Barker State Historical Center Collection.

Ford, John S. "Mrs. Alsbury's Recollections of the Fall of the Alamo." Ford Collection, Barker Center for American History. Austin: University of Texas, 1886.

Green, Rena Maverick, editor. *Memoirs of Mary A. Maverick*. San Antonio: Alamo Printing Co., 1921.

Pena, Jose Enrique de la. *With Santa Anna in Texas: A Personal Narrative of the Revolution*. Translated and edited by Carmen Perry. College Station: Texas A&M University Press, 1975.

Ragsdale, Crystal Sasse. *Women and Children of the Alamo*. Austin: State House Press, 1994.

San Antonio Daily Express, July 1888; November 1902; May 1907.

Urrea, Jose de. "General Jose Urrea's Diary, February–March 1836." *Handbook of Texas Online*: www.tamu.edu/faculty/ccbn.

Velasco-Marquez, Jesus. "A Mexican Viewpoint on the War with the United States." San Diego: *La Prensa*, 1998.

Voices of Mexico, vol. 41. Mexico City: Center for Research on North America, University of Mexico, 1997.

CHAPTER 3: SUSAN SHELBY MAGOFFIN

Inman, Henry. *The Old Santa Fe Trail.* Topeka, KS: Crane & Company, 1916.

Kansas City Star, October 8, 1926.

Magoffin, Susan Shelby. *Down the Santa Fe Trail and into Mexico.* New Haven, CT: Yale University Press, 1926.

CHAPTER 4: FRANCES BOYD

Boyd, Orsemus. *Cavalry Life in Tent & Field*. Lincoln: University of Nebraska Press, 1894.

Brown, Dee. *The Gentle Tamers: Women of the Old Wild West.* Lincoln: University of Nebraska Press, 1958.

Clan Boyd Society website, The Boyd Family Information Center: http://clanboyd.info.

Handbook of Texas Online: www.scotweb.co.uk/info/boyd. Austin: University of Texas, 1997–2000.

Reiter, Joan S. *The Women*. New York: The Time Life Series, 1979.

Summerhayes, Martha. *Vanished Arizona: Recollections of the Army Life of a New England Woman*. Lincoln: University of Nebraska Press, 1888.

CHAPTER 5: CATHY WILLIAMS

Clarke, Charles. "Cathay Williams Story." *St. Louis Daily Times*, January 2, 1876.

Dobak, William A. "Buffalo Soldiers: Separating Fact from Legend." *Wild West Magazine*, April 2003.

Fowler, Arlen L. *The Black Infantry in the West, 1869–1891.* Norman: University of Oklahoma Press, 1996.

McKenna, Morris A. *The Black West.* Cheyenne: Wyoming Leads Press, 1972.

Thompson, Melodie. "Only a Woman: Female Buffalo Soldier Cathay Williams." *National Museum of American History,* March 2001.

Tucker, Phillip T. *Cathy Williams: From Slave to Female Buffalo Soldier.* Mechanicsburg, PA: Stackpole Books, 2002.

Williams, Mary. "Cathay Williams Female Buffalo Soldier." *Fort Davis National Historical Society,* October 20, 2002.

CHAPTER 6: CHARLEY HATFIELD

Colorado Transcript, Golden, CO, January–March 1885.

Daily Chronicle, Leadville, CO, July 15, 1879.

Hall, Richard. *Patriots in Disguise: Women Warriors of the Civil War.* New York: Marlowe & Company, 1993.

Hattaway, Herman. *Historical Times Illustrated Encyclopedia of the Civil War.* New York: Harper & Row, 1986.

Mazzulla, Fred M., and William Kostka. *Mountain Charley or the Adventures of Mrs. E. J. Guerin.* Norman: University of Oklahoma Press, 1968.

Rocky Mountain News, Denver, CO, September 10, 1859.

CHAPTER 7: WINEMA

Goodrich, Thomas. *Indian Wars.* Mechanicsburg, PA: Stackpole Books, 1997.

Meacham, Hon. A. B. *Winema and Her People.* Hartford, CT: American Publishing Company, 1876.

Paul, Jan. "Modoc Bushwhack Peace Commissioners." *Chronicle of the Old West* 3, no. 35 (April 2003).

White, Julia. "Kaitchkona Winema—Modoc." Women's Spirit website: www.powersource.com/gallery/womensp/default. html.

CHAPTER 8: ELIZABETH CUSTER

Custer, Elizabeth B. *Boots and Saddles.* New York: Harper & Brothers, 1885.

_____. "Home Making in the American Army." *Harper's Bazaar,* September 22, 1900.

Dippie, Brian W. *Custer's Last Stand: Anatomy of an American Myth.* Lincoln: University of Nebraska Press, 1976.

Leckie, Shirley. *Elizabeth Bacon Custer and the Making of a Myth.* Norman: University of Oklahoma Press, 1993.

McClelland, John B. *History of Monroe County, Michigan.* 2 vols. Chicago: Lewis Publishing, 1913.

"A Moment in Time." *Kansas State Historical Society,* June 1995.

Utley, Robert M. *Custer: Cavalier in Buckskin.* Norman: University of Oklahoma Press, 1997.

CHAPER 9: LOZEN

Adams, Alexandra B. *Geronimo: A Biography.* New York: De Capo Press, 1971.

Aleshire, Peter. *Warrior Woman: The Story of Lozen, Apache Warrior and Shaman.* New York: St. Martin's Press, 2001.

Lockwood, Frank. *The Apache Indians.* Lincoln: University of Nebraska Press, 1938.

Reflections of the West Magazine 10, no. 15 (March 1993).

Schwatka, Frederick. *Among the Apaches.* Palmer Lake, CO: The Filter Press, 1974.

White, Julia. *Woman Spirit: Lozen Chiricahua Apache.* Pierre, SD: Herman Press, 1996.

CHAPTER 10: SARAH WINNEMUCCA

Alta California, April 14, 1861; October 22, 1864.

Bozeman Chronicle, October 28, 1891; November 18, 1891.

Daily Silver State, March 16, 1872; March 16 and 29, 1875.

Davison, Stanley R., editor. "The Bannock-Piute War of 1878: Letters of Major Edwin C. Mason." *Journal of the West*, Los Angeles, January 1972.

Elko Independent, September 22, 1887; October 22, 1887.

Hein, O. L. *Memories of Long Ago*. New York: G. P. Putnam, 1925.

Hopkins, Sarah Winnemucca. *Life Among the Piutes: Their Wrongs and Claims* (1883). Reno: University of Nevada Press, 1994.

Jocelyn, Stephen Perry. *Mostly Alkali*. Caldwell, ID: Caxton Printers, 1953.

Nevada State Journal, February 12, 1873.

Oregon Historical Quarterly, June 1969.

Reno Evening Gazette, June 26, 1885.

San Francisco Call, November 22 and 26, 1879; December 5, 6, and 7, 1879; October 18, 1883; January 22, 1885; February 4, 11, and 22, 1885.

San Francisco Chronicle, November 23 and 26, 1879; December 7, 9, 21, and 24, 1879.

Territorial Enterprise, January 9 and 27, 1878; May 18 and 22, 1878; June 11, 13, 14, 22, 28, and 30, 1878; July 17, 18, and 28, 1878; November 15, 1878.

Thompson, William. "Reminiscences of a Pioneer." *Alturas Plain Dealer*, San Francisco, 1912.

Zanjani, Sally. *Sarah Winnemucca*. Lincoln: University of Nebraska Press, 2001.

CHAPTER 11: CALAMITY JANE

Belle Fourche Bulletin, January 23, 1896; January 15, 1903.

Black Hills Daily Times, October 5, 1895.

Brink, Elizabeth A. "Clothing Calamity Jane, an Exercise in Historical Research." *True West*, 1990.

Burk, Martha Jane Canary. *Life and Adventures of Calamity Jane, By Herself.* 1896.

Daily Press and Dakotian, December 18, 1877.

Deadwood Pioneer, July 13, 1876.

Free Press, January 13, 1883.

McClintock, John S. *Pioneer Days in the Black Hills* (1939). Norman: University of Oklahoma Press, 2000.

McLaird, James D. "Calamity Jane's Diaries and Letters." *Montana Magazine* 45 (1995).

Midland Mail, November 14, 1929.

Pioneer-Review, June 15, 1939.

Pioneer Times, August 2 and 6, 1903.

Rand County Press, December 6, 1882.

Ray, Grace Ernestine. *Wily Women of the West*. San Antonio: Naylor Company, 1972.

Sioux Falls Argus-Leader, July 9, 1906.

Sollid, Roberta Beed. *Calamity Jane, a Study in Historical Criticism*. Helena: Historical Society of Montana, 1958.

CHAPTER 12: JULIET FISH NICHOLS

Alta California, January 11, 1869.

Clifford, Mary Louise, and J. Candace Clifford. *Women Who Kept the Lights: An Illustrated History of Female Lighthouse Keepers*. Alexandria, VA: Cypress Communications, 1994.

Daily Morning Call, June 2, 1854; November 5, 1888.

Fleming, Candace. *Women of the Lights*. Morton Grove, IL: Albert Whitman & Co., 1995.

Gallant, Clifford. "Emily Fish, The Socialite Keeper." *The Keepers Log*, spring 1985.

Gibbs, James A. Jr. *Sentinels of the North Pacific*. Portland, OR: Binfords & Mort, 1955.

Nelson, Ted, and Sharlene Nelson. *California Lighthouses*. Seattle: Umbrella Books, 1993.

"Only Yesterday." *The Keeper's Log*, fall 1996. United States Lighthouse Society, San Francisco.

Putnam, George R. "Beacons of the Sea." *National Geographic Magazine*, Washington, DC, 1913.

San Francisco Chronicle, November 10, 1895.

Shanks, Ralph, and Lisa Woo Shanks. *Guardians of the Golden Gate*. San Anselmo, CA: Costano Books, 1990.

Shanks, Ralph C. Jr., and Janetta Thompson Shanks. *Lighthouses of San Francisco Bay*. San Anselmo, CA: Costano Books, 1976.

Stumbo, Jean Serpell. *Emily Fish, Socialite Lighthouse Keeper*. Monterey, CA: Pacific Grove Museum of Natural History Association, 1997.

CHAPTER 13: PAULINE CUSHMAN

Ames Intelligencer, October 26, 1893.

Arizona Republican, March 24, 1941.

Arizona Republican, April 18, 1961.

Arizona Weekly Entertainment, December 7, 1893.

Casa Grande Bulletin, March 31, 1923.

Casa Grande Dispatch, August 20, 1995.

Centralia Daily Sentinel, November 29, 1893.

The Charleston Mercury, July 6, 1864.

Christen, William. *Pauline Cushman: Spy of the Cumberland*. Edinborough, England: Edinborough Press, 2006.

Cushman, Pauline, and F. L. Sarmiento. *Life of Pauline Cushman: The Celebrated Union Spy & Scout*. New York, NY. Big Byte Books, 2014.

Daily Leader, October 31, 1893.

Horn, Stanley F. "Dr. John Rolfe Hudson & the Confederate Underground in Nashville." *Tennessee Quarterly* 22, no. 3. Nashville, TN: March 1963.

Janesville Weekly Gazette, June 24, 1864.

Quebbeman, Frances E. *Medicine in Territorial Arizona*. Tucson: University of Arizona, 1966.

Rolfe Reveille, January 31, 1889.

San Francisco Call, December 5, 1893.

San Francisco Chronicle, April 19, 1893.

San Francisco Chronicle, December 3, 1893.

San Francisco Daily Alta, March 9, 1872.

Sherr, Lynn. *The American Woman's Gazette*. New York, NY: Bantam Book, 1976.

INDEX

About the Authors

Chris Enss is an author, scriptwriter, and comedienne who has written for television and film and performed on cruise ships and on stage. She has worked with award-winning musicians, writers, directors, and producers, and as a screenwriter for Tricor Entertainment, but her passion is for telling the stories of the men and women who shaped the history and mythology of the American West. Some of the most famous names in history, not to mention film and popular culture, populate her books. She's written or co-written more than two dozen books for TwoDot. She lives in Grass Valley, California.

JoAnn Chartier is a former broadcast journalist and talk-show host whose writing had earned regional and national awards. She lives in Oregon.